OLD MONEY, NEW WOMAN

OLD MONEY, NEW WOMAN

How To Manage Your Money and Your Life

BYRON TULLY

ACORN STREET PRESS

Contents

Old Money, New Woman: How to Manage Your Money and Your Life

Byron Tully

Acorn Street Press

Cover Photo by Gordon Parks. License courtesy of Getty Images.
Unless otherwise noted, all interior photos by Weatherford Bradley. Copyright 2016.
Interior Layout: MartinPublishingServices.com

ISBN: 978-1-950118-00-7 (hardback), 978-1-950118-01-4 (paperback)

Acknowledgements

John Donne once said that no man is an island. He might have also added that no author really writes alone.

This is doubly true when a man writes something for or about women. Obviously, as the author of this book, I have gleaned information and gained perspective from the women in my life. More importantly, I have been inspired by them.

To not acknowledge this would be negligent, if not criminal. So let me begin…

To Lark Ireland, my dear friend who provided the original idea for this book.

To Lorna Scott, whose very British grace and reserve remain sterling.

To Candyce Spruel, whose 'sisterhood', friendship, and support have been invaluable.

To Simonne Adellcia Bogel, who laughs so easily, cooks so brilliantly, and gives so freely.

To the 'girls' from my class at DPHS—Annie & Annie, Barbara, Dana, Darla, Dr. Deb, Gina, Leslie, Patti, Rae, and Shi Shi—who have been the beating heart of fun and friendship for over 40 years.

Aux filles du Fou: Carol, Noémie, Sana, et Marie—dont la générosité, la gentillesse et le café—ont rendu possible la création de ce livre.

À tous mes amis du St. Regis, pour leurs paroles aimables et leur soutien.

A Elisabetta, Ketty, e Chiarastella—i miei cari amici veronese.

And to my mother, who has been a source of patience, generosity, and above all, love.

Thank you all.

To my wife,
the Exemplar who inspires,
for her enormous contribution
to this book, and to our lives.

"And the day came when the risk to remain tight in a bud was more painful than the risk it took to blossom."

—Anais Nin

June 6, 2017—Ponferrada, Spain

Introduction

As a woman, you are the one who earns, manages, spends, and invests your money. You may be at a disadvantage in some instances, but you are not a victim. You are not helpless. You are in the driver's seat. Make no mistake about it: in a capitalist society, money is power. While you may be reading this and be under a mountain of credit card or student debt, you can turn your situation around with the application of some personal finance fundamentals. All it takes is some awareness, some choices, and some time.

Byron Tully

After the success of 'The Old Money Book' and 'The Old Money Guide To Marriage', I thought it would be beneficial—and timely—to write a book specifically for women. To that end, the purpose of this book is to educate, empower, and inspire women toward a greater level of independence and a higher quality of life.

Note that I didn't say 'help' women. Women have the intellect, resourcefulness, and drive to help themselves, thank you very much. What they often seek are new perspectives, strategies, and tools they can consider, absorb, and implement to achieve their goals in a world in which men make most of the rules...and change those rules to suit them. To that end, this book has very definitive aims:

- to encourage women to create employment and financial opportunities for themselves that will lead to financial independence for them and their families;
- to secure a social standing for women equal to men; and
- to identify and discard outdated and unhelpful social norms and social conditioning and replace them with new perspectives and new ways of thinking.

The irony that this book for women has been written by a man is not lost on me. Rather than view my gender as a (very sexist) basis upon which to discount the validity of the concepts presented here, you might consider it advantageous to learn from a man who genuinely likes women and wants them to succeed in this world.

Furthermore, it is important to acknowledge that much of this modern world has been conceived, built, and coded by men and for men, sometimes to the detriment of women. Getting insight from the inside—or the other side—however you want to view me—could prove valuable.

I wrote this for you, the modern woman who sees her life as an opportunity and an adventure. It just so happens that some of the tools at your disposal to maximize this present moment are found in time-tested traditions from the past. You may agree with the ideas I present and use some of them. You may disagree with some of the ideas and never use any of them. You may tweak some of the strategies so they are more effective for you. I am very realistic about my place in your life. I am not the authority: you are. Only you know what you need to improve, what motivates you, and what you are really willing to do to change your situation.

Still, the bottom-line benefit of this book will remain: it will give you the opportunity to become more aware, more informed, and be able to make better choices. These concepts and strategies will help you navigate waters that are still sexist, still misogynistic, still unfair, and still violent. To be clear, I don't advocate a 'war of the sexes' or a hostile attitude toward men, or anyone for that matter. I advocate an open, communicative, deliberate, and balanced approach to dealing with life and the people in it, including men.

There is a legendary prayer by Reinhold Niebuhr in which he asks the Lord to grant him the serenity to accept the things he can't change, the courage to change the things he can, and the wisdom to know the difference. It's called the Serenity Prayer. To the contrary, I'm going to present concepts that I think you, as a woman, will be best served to challenge, or to find a way to circumvent. My gift to you is to articulate what some of these choices and issues are. Your charge is to address them as best you can.

I'm going to eschew the popular label 'feminist'. I believe that everyone on the planet should be treated with equal respect and given equal opportunity regardless of their gender, race, sexual preference, ethnicity, or religion. I'm going to reference the culture I know best: Old Money.

'Old Money' is a term that generally refers to individuals and families who've enjoyed wealth and privilege for three generations or more. You're probably familiar with the term, and may even know a few people who've been referred to as Old Money. I'm going to articulate the rarely discussed, almost secret traditions of Old Money that you, as a woman, can use in school, at work, at home, in your own personal situation, to live a richer life in the modern world. I'm not going to tell you what to do. I'm going to share with you concepts and strategies I've seen work well, generation after generation.

To be clear, your current socioeconomic status does not matter. Your current net worth does not matter. Your current age does not matter. What matters is your desire to join what has been called 'the true nobility'. That is, to endeavor to be a better person tomorrow than you are today.

To join that nobility is a journey. This book can, quite simply, prepare you for that journey.

So, please take a moment and politely but firmly shut out the noisy turmoil all around you. Pull focus on yourself, your world, your goals, and your dreams. Let's see what we can do to maximize those, right here, right now, with the resources we have to work with. We may not be able to see all the way to the horizon, but we can find a way forward in the visible distance ahead.

To the journey...

Byron Tully

November, 2018

"Whatever you can do or dream you can—begin it. Boldness has genius, power, and magic in it."

—Goethe

CHAPTER 1

A Room With A View

Goethe had it right. Get started. Move. Grow. Begin it. So let's begin this journey by taking a moment to understand the importance of perspective. Perspective can be defined as the viewpoint or viewpoints you have when you look at something. It certainly affects *how* you look at something and *what* you see when you look at it. What many women don't realize is that perspective may affect whether you *actually see something at all.*

What you look at, or consider, can be a tangible, solid object like a table or a piece of art. It can also be a concept, i.e., your life. Your personal experience, education, or religious beliefs may inform your perspective on a concept. Acquiring more information, meeting new people, having different experiences, and speaking with others about a concept may change your perspective—and your choices.

In this context, perspective affects, among other things, *when* you do the things you do, (specifically, at what point in your life you make important choices), and *how* these choices fit into the big picture.

Let's say, as an exaggerated example, that you live your entire life in your bedroom. You never leave it and only see the outside world through a single window. You have no idea what the rest of your house looks like. You have less of an idea about your neighborhood, and no idea about your world. You make choices based on your existence in your bedroom, not your life in the world, because you have seen the world only from the perspective of your bedroom.

This illustrates a lack of perspective. The person living only in their bedroom can be compared to a person who sees their life only in the present moment, not where they are in relation to their entire life. It also can refer to a person who has not read, studied, learned, traveled, or experienced very much: their perspective is limited. They can't see things in context, whether it's geographic, cultural, or historical. On a personal level, they don't understand that the choices they make today affect their lives over the long term.

Living life can provide you some 'perspective' as you gain (sometimes painful) experience and (hard won) knowledge. Still, it is essential to start the journey with a sense of 'perspective'. That is, the ability to see things in context, in their relationship to other things, and to the whole. In this chapter, we address these 'things' as major choices you make or options you have as you go through life, which is the 'whole' in question.

Here's a simple exercise to help with perspective: take a piece of paper and turn it horizontally. Take a pen and draw a straight line across the page, going from right to left. Write 'zero' at the left end of the line and 85 on the far right end of the line.

Now, as you proceed from 'zero to 85', at proportionate intervals, write 18, 30, 45, and 65. As you might have guessed, this is a primitive chronology of your life, from birth to 85 years of age. Before we go into detail about each option point, or 'tentpole', that may occur in your life around the ages of 18, 30, 45, and 65, let's look at some foundational building blocks in the life of an Old Money Gal (OMG).

'You cannot easily fit women into a structure that is already coded for men.'

–Cathy O'Neil

Perspective and The Old Money Gal

When it comes to gaining perspective on their lives and using that perspective to make good decisions, an Old Money Gal has a few obvious advantages. They include:

- a social network with resources and information that provides exposure and feeds understanding;
- finances that provide her more choices when considering a career, or choosing to not work in a conventional sense;
- the time to observe and reflect, as her household is a generally tranquil and predictable environment; and
- the lives of her accomplished ancestors which are held up as examples.

Old Money families tend to promote and reinforce structure: doing certain things at certain points in time in life. The young Old Money Gal attends prep school growing up. She then goes to college. If she wants to take a gap year and backpack across the country or live abroad, she does that. Then, she goes to work in her chosen profession. At a certain point, she may get married, and if she decides to, she has children.

Disruptions or deviations from this norm are rare. Events like unplanned pregnancies or dropping out of high school are almost nonexistent. There's a pattern, and she usually follows it. Why? Because it makes sense and has yielded very good results for past generations. If something works, why rebel against it? Why try to 'fix' it?

The Old Money Gal observes her parents, grandparents, and extended family, and has a chance to see their lives in comparison to her own: where she's been, where she is, where she wants to go. She benefits from witnessing and sharing in their active, deliberately paced, well-considered, and thoughtful way of life. At an early age, she gains perspective.

Still, she faces the same challenges you do in deciding *what* to do, if not *when* to do it. She also faces the same chauvinist attitudes held by men who'd prefer she stay home and grill a good steak rather than go out into the world and contribute to it mightily. She has advantages, but she is not immune to obstacles.

~ OLD MONEY SECRET ~

Perspective, the vantage point from which you view something, may be the most important piece of information you can have about a choice. It's important to acquire and maintain perspective. The best decisions about what to do and when to do it are made with a sense of perspective.

* * * * * * * *

THINGS TO REMEMBER

A big advantage in life is to gain perspective on 'life in general' prior to making plans for 'your life' in particular. That's why this chapter on perspective is the first chapter in this book: to help you see your present, personal situation from a slightly removed, more objective viewpoint, in the context of the whole. This might reduce the pressure of any pending choice or decision you might have right now that you may think is the biggest decision ever. It may very well be a big decision, but seeing it in the 'birth to age 85' context might, yes, 'put it in perspective'. Now, look at your situation and ask yourself these questions:

- Do you have a social network of family, friends, mentors, and colleagues that provides you reliable information, emotional support, and current resources to help you get and maintain perspective on your life and the major choices you face?
- Are your finances in order? Or are they a distraction, burden, or obstacle to you as you attempt to prioritize things in the short term and plan for the long term?
- Have you structured your daily or weekly schedule to allow yourself quiet time to reflect on your life?
- Do you have role models whose lives provide points of reference and inspiration to you?

Answering these questions honestly and then taking a first step to correct or improve them is critical. Remember the quote from Goethe that began this book and this chapter: 'Whatever you can do or dream you can, begin it'—so begin. Take this small inventory. Decide what you can improve and how you can start the process. After you've done that, we'll look at some common, important choices you'll probably have in your life and discuss how to address them.

So expand your 'room with a view'. See your life with perspective. See your life as a journey. Then begin the journey.

Introducing The Exemplars

Sometimes it's difficult to have perspective on your own life. It may help to look at someone else's life and see what parallels can be drawn between the situation you're in, and the challenges you face, and the life someone else lived, and the challenges they faced.

To that end, at the end of each chapter we're going to highlight the life of a great woman. These are sterling examples—Exemplars. Explore the lives of these remarkable women who changed history. Read their biographies. Learn about the challenges they faced. Be inspired by their accomplishments. Emulate their best qualities. Honor their legacies.

'Challenge your assumptions
so you can find your truth.'

–Anonymous

Exemplar – Madame Curie

Marie Sklodowska Curie was born in Warsaw, Poland, on November 7, 1867. The daughter of a secondary schoolteacher, Marie went to Paris to study physics and mathematics at the Sorbonne in 1891. There she met Pierre Curie, professor of the School of Physics, whom she married in 1895.

Together, the Curies began investigating radioactivity, and in July 1898, they announced the discovery of a new chemical element, polonium. Soon thereafter, they announced the discovery of another, radium. The couple, along with Henri Becquerel, was awarded the Nobel Prize for Physics in 1903 for their work on radioactivity.

Following the tragic death of her husband Pierre in 1906, Madame Curie took over his teaching post, becoming the first woman to teach at the Sorbonne University. She devoted herself to continuing the work that they had begun together. In 1911 Madame Curie won another Nobel Prize in Chemistry for creating a means for measuring radioactivity.

Her research and work remained largely in the domain of the academic until the First World War when she applied her discoveries to the development of x-rays in surgery. During the war, she designed and equipped small ambulances with mobile X-ray units. These were used to diagnose injuries near the front lines.

The International Red Cross made her head of its radiological service and she held training courses for medical orderlies and doctors. As Director of the Red Cross Radiological Service, she toured Paris, raising money and seeking donations of supplies and vehicles which could be converted to ambulances.

In October 1914, these first X-ray machines, known as "Petits Curies", were ready, and Madame Curie set off to the front. Her daughter Irene, then aged 17, joined her at casualty clearing stations close to the front lines, X-raying wounded men to locate fractures, bullets and shrapnel. Madame Curie's expertise and technology saved thousands of lives.

After the war, she continued her work as a researcher, teacher and head of a laboratory. Despite her accomplishments and contributions, Madame Curie still faced great opposition from male scientists in France and never received significant financial rewards from her work.

By the late 1920s her health was beginning to deteriorate. She died on July 4, 1934, from leukemia, caused by exposure to high-energy radiation from her research. She was the first woman to be interred at the Pantheon in Paris. The Curies' eldest daughter Irene became a scientist as well, and also won the Nobel Prize for Chemistry.

Madame Curie's discoveries and innovations changed the landscape of science and medicine forever.

If you see science, technology, and medicine as beautiful endeavors waiting to be explored, learn more about the life and work of Madame Curie.

"We must have perseverance and above all confidence in ourselves. We must believe that we are gifted for something and that this thing must be attained."

—Marie Curie

"Do or do not. There is no try."

—Confucius

May 26, 2017—San Juan, Spain

CHAPTER 2

The Greatest Show on Earth

If you've ever visited the circus when it came to town, or if you've seen a circus tent, you'll remember the shape of it: its large canvas sheets are supported by tentpoles—round pillars that hold up the covering and give it form and structure. The more sturdy and well-placed the tentpoles, the more secure the circus tent.

Let's look at your life as a circus tent. We'll look at the 'tentpoles' and define those as option points or big choices that define how the canvas of your life takes shape and turns out. While every woman's journey is unique in the smaller events, challenges, and choices she faces, these tentpoles are major moments many women experience. The choices that accompany them have a large and often permanent impact. They can determine how sturdy and secure the canvas of your life is.

Refer now to your '18 to 85' chart.

Your First Tentpole will probably occur around the age of 18, when you graduate from high school and have the choice to continue your education in college or other institution of higher learning.

Your Second Tentpole will probably occur around the age of 30, when you decide whether or not you're going to have children and be a parent.

Your Third Tentpole will probably occur around the age of 45, when you've established yourself in your career and have choices about what you can do with your resources such as experience, expertise, financial independence, influence, and time.

Your Fourth Tentpole will probably occur around the age of 65, when you have the opportunity to retire, continue working, or transition to some different kind of endeavor.

Note: you will have many decisions to make in life. These are just a few of the big ones. The 'ages' of 18, 30, 45, and 65 that I've assigned to these options are, of course, variable from woman to woman. I've selected these, not at random, but because they are common approximate chronological markers for these tentpoles. Let's take a look at them in more detail.

Your First Tentpole

This tentpole occurs around the age of 18. *This may be the first time in your life that you make a big decision about your life.* Your choices at this point can be to continue your formal education or end it with a high school diploma. You can choose to get the best job you can with the education you have, maybe as a waitress or file clerk, or you can choose to enroll in an institution of higher learning. Choose wisely.

It's important to acknowledge that you've probably spent most of your childhood and adolescence financially and emotionally dependent on someone else. You've been growing up and learning about life, in school and from your environment. On the day you turn 18, you are legally an adult, but you've spent 95% of your life as a child. Unless you've had an extraordinary childhood, you aren't really equipped to make big decisions consistently well.

Terminating your education, going into the workforce, or getting married and/or getting pregnant at this age are big steps. You *can* be an employee or parent at the age of 18, or even younger. The real question is: do you have the emotional, vocational, and financial resources to do those two things well over the long haul?

As a job applicant and future employee, your job prospects for the present and the future may be limited with only a high school education. There may be opportunities to learn on the job as you work and progress, but other candidates with more education will be competing for those promotions as well.

If you decide to begin a family immediately, you become responsible for yourself and a child. You also become involved with other adults (the father of the child, for example) for the rest of your life. If you don't have any long-term experience being responsible for yourself, is it wise to introduce another responsibility—a lifetime one, at that—right now?

It is also important to consider what happens if you *postpone a decision* at this point in your life. If you postpone starting to work or starting a family, you can always make a decision to do that later. If you postpone your education, you may never get back to it, especially if you start a family.

Furthermore, it's important to consider what happens if you *make a mistake* at this point. If you make a mistake about starting a family, it is one you live with for the rest of your life. If you make a mistake about, let's say, the college you choose to attend, you can always change your mind and transfer to another college. You can make a decision—and a mistake—about both of these. Only one will be an irrevocable decision that permanently changes the trajectory of your life.

Note: many people want to get married. Not everybody is prepared to be married. Many people want to have a baby. Not everyone is prepared to be a parent. Babies are cute. Children are work.

I suggest you continue your education. Even if you may not know what you want to do with your life, getting an education will help you as you move toward making that decision. It will introduce you to possibilities and give you resources and exposure to take advantage of those possibilities.

Make this *investment* in yourself, to mature as a person and to develop a skill set and social network you can use in your chosen profession. It may be a two-year technical college, a four-year university, or six or eight years that include post-graduate studies.

Whatever form it takes, it's important to see a college education as a transformational journey. You start it as an 18 year old adolescent, at the mercy of economic conditions and confined by a limited worldview. You complete it as a twenty-something young adult with core knowledge, social and vocational skills, self-discipline, and some exposure to a larger world under your belt.

Know that your education, in any sense of the word, has just begun. At the age of 18, you've learned to read, write, and understand basic math and science. You have a general understanding about history and the world around you.

That's not a large reservoir to draw upon if you want to max out this personal opportunity—your life. I encourage you to get the best education you can. You will learn *facts and skills*, but, more importantly, you will learn *how to improve and refine your decision-making processes.* The implications and impact of education cannot be overstated, as it informs and enriches each tentpole that follows.

Note: Old Money Gals prioritize education. It is an experience that 'rounds them out' as young women. It introduces them to a new world (a college campus), to new people (professors and fellow students), and to new ideas (found in the textbooks, lectures, and conversations). It is invaluable.

'Never be too big to ask questions.
Never know too much to learn something new.'

—Og Mandingo

Your Second Tentpole

This occurs around the age of 30. This is the time you consider whether or not to have children and to be a parent for the rest of your life.

Please note that I say 'you consider' whether or not to have children. This implies that you have a conversation, first with yourself and then with your partner, about being a parent. You think about it. You discuss it. You weigh the advantages and disadvantages. *You search the midnight of your soul,* as the poets say. Then you decide. Then you plan.

Let's say you have spent ages 18 to 23 getting an education, and ages 24 to 30 working and experiencing life as an independent adult. You have found a partner in life. You are in a committed relationship or married. You are financially stable, if not financially independent or wealthy. Now, you feel that you may be ready for children.

Much undue social pressure can be bought to bear on young women during this time. They are often expected to get married and have children, even in this quote-unquote modern age. Be aware of this pressure and have the courage to make up your own mind about when, if, and with whom you start a family. There is no stigma, and often much more freedom and many more options in life, love, and work, for women who do not have children.

To have the most choices in life, it's important to avoid so-called 'accidents' that can disrupt or destroy your plans, hopes, and dreams for the future. With regards to pregnancy, there are no 'accidents'. Unplanned pregnancy is a consequence of ignorance, carelessness, bad decision-making, or a combination of the three. Sperm plus egg equals pregnancy. It's that simple and, for the unprepared, a harsh reality.

In charting your own course as a modern woman, it is important to understand that the responsibility of birth control should be shared. However, the harsh reality in most instances is that it is completely your responsibility. Unless you want to be a parent, make sure you take precautions yourself. When a pregnancy occurs and you decide to be a parent, the responsibility of raising that child will be primarily yours, regardless of what your partner says or how well-intentioned he is.

Unfair? You betcha. Inaccurate? Hardly. Likely to change in your lifetime? Doubtful. Best to know it and plan accordingly? Bingo, Ringo. Understand that the planet is overpopulated as it is. If you want to live your life for yourself and/or your partner, don't have children. I've heard it's very thrilling to be pregnant, exhilarating to give birth, and joyful to care for a newborn. Family members and friends offer congratulations, celebrations, and support. *You*, as a new mother, are the center of attention.

Then, not long after that, family and friends all go on with their lives and *you* get to wake up at 3 a.m. and change a diaper, feed the growing child, and comfort it when it cries. Don't be resentful if this life shock puts the brakes on some of your goals and plans, hobbies, and interests. Don't be surprised if you dream of just sleeping 8 hours in a row, forget starting a new business.

The decision to become a parent is so critically important that I must take a little extra time and ask you to do something for me, and for yourself, at this tentpole. *Do a little research.* Assess statistics that correlate teen pregnancy with limited economic and educational opportunities for women, with poverty, with complications involved in childbirth, and with childhood diseases.

Ask women you know who are parents to confide in you: of course they love their children, but, if they had it to do all over again, would they still be a parent? Would they have had children as early as they did? Would they have the same number of children? Ask women with infants. Ask women in high school who have children. Ask women with adult children. Listen carefully to what they say. Listen even more carefully to what they don't say. And be sure to ask *the women*, the mothers. The men may or may not have their careers and lives impacted by the birth and raising of children. The woman certainly will. The women certainly do. Be honest with yourself and be honest with your partner before you get married. The question is not: do you want to have children one day? The question is: *do you want to be a parent for the rest of your life?*

Don't think that when a child turns 18 or 21 years of age that your job is done. They will turn to you when they are 30, when they are 50, and even when you are 90. They will need your emotional support, your guidance, and may even need your financial assistance. They may have children of their own. You may help them parent. You will be a grandparent, but it is possible that you may become a parent to your grandchildren, willingly or not.

I know couples that absolutely love being parents. They are loving and fully engaged raising their children, committing time and money, prioritizing and planning. Other couples don't have the energy and commitment to be really good parents. Some start off overwhelmed, but then grow into it, finding the discipline to meet their responsibilities. Others, disinterested, unprepared, and soon defeated by the demands, do the bare minimum or not even that.

It's perfectly fine to be the barista at the neighborhood coffee shop while you're studying and working toward your goals. It's much more challenging to be the barista who's working and trying to figure out how to afford day care, orthodontics, and soccer uniforms for your child. A happy, healthy, and productive life requires a plan. A plan is to have a career, probably two, and some money in the bank that will be sufficient to care for yourselves and address the needs of your child. A plan acknowledges that somebody's career is going to have to take a backseat while raising the child for a period of time, and you never know how long that's going to be. A plan is realistic: if you look at your situation as a couple and don't see how you could afford a pet, how the hell do you think you can afford a child? If you can't afford to raise a child, don't have a child. '*We'll figure it out when the time comes*' is not a plan.

Being a parent has always been challenging. Children's access to the internet and social media makes the job even more demanding today. The world is a minefield. Children are miracles. Know this. Consider this. This period, ages 24 to 30, can be a great time in life, full of opportunities to travel, have a career, enjoy financial freedom and great relationships. Keep your options open, your possibilities growing. You have choices. I'm not telling you what to do, but I am telling you what to think: think about everything, over a lifetime, before you make this decision. It is irreversible.

By waiting to approximately the age of 30 to consider having children, you have given yourself several advantages. Here are just a few:

- You've given yourself time to grow up.
- You've given yourself time to get an education.
- You've given yourself time to get on your feet financially.
- You've given yourself time to enjoy life as an adult, on your own.
- You've given yourself time to meet and develop a solid relationship with another person who will, most likely, share the joy and challenges of raising a child.

You want, and probably need, all of these advantages.

Your Third Tentpole

This occurs around the age of 45. At this juncture, you may have been working for 20 years.

If you have children, they could be in high school or just starting college. It might be that you're committed to pay for their education. It might be the first time you have the house to yourself, or the first time in a long time you have your partner to yourself. You may have a certain amount of freedom and a moment in which to reflect. At this moment in your life, you may have the chance to change directions, downsize, relocate, expand your social circle, go back to school, or rededicate your efforts to your work. If your career has been a priority, the coming period between ages 45 and 65 could be your most productive and rewarding, both personally and financially. You may have climbed the corporate ladder or be in private practice.

You may have secured your credentials. You may have mastered the fundamentals of your profession and even its finer points. Your network of colleagues could be well-developed. Your position in your industry and your community might be established. You could have credibility, perhaps influence, perhaps affluence.

During this time, you can mentor. You can teach. You can write. You can impart your wisdom, bootstrap other women's and men's careers, give to charity, or start a charity. This is a moment you may have the freedom, resources, experience, and vision to soar in any direction you choose.

Where do you want to be? What position do you want to be in career-wise? Financially? Personally? Is this the time you'd like to jump ship and start a second career? Go into business for yourself? Take that 'gap' year off and live in a foreign country? Volunteer in your community?

All these things may seem very far away and almost impossible to attain if, right now, you're a college senior with a mountain of student debt and shaky job prospects or a 30-something mom with a desire to do more. But I will tell you this: time flies. I will also tell you quite honestly that you can do almost anything you want to do. What is required most often is that you:

- get the idea in your head;
- figure out what needs to be done;
- organize your resources;
- develop necessary skills;
- work toward your goal consistently;
- learn from your mistakes, and;
- never quit.

Again, set a tangible goal. Know what's required to achieve it. Get your ducks in a row. Do the work. Improve. Persevere. Achieve one goal. Then the next. You'll astonish yourself.

Your Fourth Tentpole

This occurs around the age of 65. You may have been working for 40 years, longer than some people you work with have been alive. You'll think of them and may refer to them as 'kids'. They'll refer to you as 'ma'am', and this may be irritating.

You may have the inclination to retire from the workforce. Your boss, if you have one, may invite you to lunch and subtly or not so subtly mention that you've had a great career and that you've made a great contribution to the company. Regardless of how successful you've been, how much money you've made, it might sting a little bit when someone directs you to the exit.

Another scenario is that you may voluntarily scale back your hours, work part-time, or quit completely. 'Retirement', I will tell you from the many friends I've known who've done it, is great. For about three months. Then boredom sets in. Even those with all the money and resources in the world choose to work even as they age. Music icon Rod Stewart, who has sold over 100 million records world-wide since he started singing in 1961, mentioned not too long ago that he gets 'anxious' after sitting around the (obviously very comfortable) house for a couple of weeks. As a person who can buy or do anything, or go anywhere and meet anyone, he just wants to go back to work, all these years later. That should tell you something.

Remember: time flies. I would suggest that you have some sort of vague idea right now about what you might like to do from the age of 65 to the age of 85. I would also suggest that you start right now: work hard at something you care about, live wisely and below your means (read 'The Old Money Book' for guidance on this). Save your money, invest astutely, and be in a position to do more than survive. You'll also want to exercise, eat right, and be happy now so you're healthy in your golden years.

The Long View

Now, let's take a moment and take a deep breath. You can't know all this stuff right now, or ever. You can't plan all this stuff. You *can* have a plan, though, and start to work on it. You *can* be aware of the span of your life and appreciate that it is finite. You should always try to maintain Your Perspective on Your Life as you meet people, set goals, accept or reject limits concerning what you think you can or cannot do, what you will or won't do, what you can or can't be.

If you're 18 years old and you think you've met the Love of Your Life and you're ready to get married, start a family, and be a mom and wife for the rest of your life, take a moment. Look at this piece of paper we've just drawn out together. Is that really the best choice you can make right now?

18 to 85. That's a long time, but it goes by quite quickly. You can learn, grow, and change tremendously…in just a year or two. Give yourself the benefit of the doubt. If you're 30 years old and single, or just married, gaze toward the horizon and imagine where you'd like to be in 15 years. With children? Without children? Different city? Different country? If you're 45, or 65, or at any point along the way, you have the chance to examine where you are, reflect upon the choices you've made, consider the goals and dreams you have and have had, and assess the resources you have at your disposal to make them a reality. If you have made a choice you're not happy with, give yourself the opportunity to make new choices. As you implement these choices into your daily life, you get to experience the rewards or consequences they bring.

Note: if you feel like you don't have options, then you aren't sufficiently aware of your situation, or you are not willing to change your habits, or both. So take a moment and get some perspective.

Things To Remember

Brief fairytale: once upon a time, a young princess was lost in the woods. She came upon a frog who wore a small gold crown on his tiny green head. 'I'm sorry to bother you,' said the princess, 'but I was walking in the woods, and now I'm lost. Can you help me get back to my castle?' 'Certainly, your highness,' said the frog. 'Do you know where your castle is?' 'Yes,' replied the princess. 'It's near the river, on the highest mountain in the land.' 'Do you know where you are now?' asked the frog. 'No, I don't,' replied the princess. To which the frog replied, 'Then you can't get there from here.'

The moral of the silly story is this: in order to get to where you want to go, you have to know where you are. Otherwise, no one, not even a prince of a frog, can give you directions. The '18 to 85' chart and our review of life's common tentpoles will help you determine where you are so you can decide how to get to where you want to be. (We'll go into more detail on 'direction' in a later chapter.)

Another concept to keep in mind and apply to many of the issues we'll discuss in this book is B.A.S.I.S. In this case, the acronym refers to the following:

> Budget—budget or limit your focus to where you think you are right now in life. Think in the short, narrow term to get started. Then broaden your field of view later.
>
> Acquire—acquire the necessary perspective to determine what the next big tentpole is for you and how you can make the best choice.
>
> Save—save your energy and apply it to competently and thoroughly executing the choice you make for your next big tentpole.
>
> Invest—invest in resources that can help you make the most of your choice.
>
> Spend—spend time in quiet reflection in order to acquire and maintain perspective on your life and to firmly establish the tentpoles that give your life shape.

Remember: "Do or do not, there is no try." Make a plan, don't *try t*o, do it.

EXEMPLAR – SONIA SOTOMAYOR

How much do you know about Sonia Sotomayor? The daughter of Puerto Rican immigrants, she is the third woman and the first Latina to sit on the Supreme Court of the United States.

At the age of 9, Justice Sotomayor's father died, leaving her mother to raise her and her brother in the Bronx—a tough working-class neighborhood of New York City. Nevertheless, she graduated first in her high school class and attended Princeton

University on full scholarship. She then attended Yale Law School on scholarship. In her third year, she filed a formal complaint against an established Washington, D.C., law firm for suggesting during a recruiting dinner that she was at Yale only because of affirmative action policies. Refusing to be interviewed by the firm, she filed her complaint with a faculty–student tribunal, which ruled in her favor. Her action triggered a campus-wide debate, and news of the firm's subsequent December 1978 apology made the *Washington Post.*

Justice Sotomayor pursued a career in private practice, but the bench called. She is the only woman to have been nominated to three different judicial positions by three different presidents, one Republican and two Democrats.

If you think you may have a career in the legal profession, I encourage you to learn more about Justice Sonia Sotomayor.

"I do know one thing about me: I don't measure myself by others' expectations or let others define my worth."

–Sonia Sotomayor

"Be yourself. Everyone else is taken."

—Oscar Wilde

May 27, 2017—Atapuerca, Spain

CHAPTER 3

It Is What You Know

If you only read one chapter in this book, read this one. It is critical. I've referenced 'being prepared for this journey'. Education is *the* vital aspect of preparation because it involves the development of your mind, your most prized possession in this world.

The importance of an education cannot be overstated. Education may be the key, fundamental experience that enables you to elevate and transform your life. It matters not what your skin color is, what religion you practice, how old you are, or where you live in the world—the effects of education are universal.

Education is your way up. It is your way out. It is your weapon. It is your shield. It is your light. It is your fire. Get it and use it. Education is yours forever. Once you have it, it can never be taken away.

Education may be described as the process by which you are introduced to new information and ideas through experience and instruction. It is also the manner in which you understand and apply new knowledge. When we refer to 'education' in this book, we will most often refer to the formal, structured system of classroom education that takes place in schools and universities. Education is often provided by teachers in a classroom. Learning is what you do for yourself throughout your lifetime.

In the United States, education is often taken for granted because of the easy access to public schools. However, in less developed regions around the world, parents work long hours in horrendous conditions doing miserable jobs in order to scrape together the money to send their children to school. They do this in India, where many families live on sixty dollars a week. Think about that. They do this in China, where a multigenerational family of six may be living in a two bedroom apartment. Think about that. They do this in Africa, where children study by kerosene lamps at night, after working all day. Think about that.

They do this because they often live in a world of crushing poverty that can be deadly. The difference between starvation and a living wage is often the margin between ignorance and education: the acquisition of basic skills and applied knowledge. The skills and knowledge that lift people out of poverty and into the middle class are almost always developed through education. The fact that people most hard-pressed to survive prioritize education should tell you something about its importance.

To fully appreciate the value of an education today—and where it can take you tomorrow—it might be good to remember where women were in the not too distant past. Throughout history, men have been able to maintain power over women because women have not been able to be self-sufficient. Generations of women have been denied an education, treated like property, unable to own property, excluded from financial decisions, and generally oppressed and cloistered by 'men-made' traditions.

Women have lived with legislation they did not help draft and that they did not vote into law. They have been marginalized, silenced, and relegated to being the bearer of children and performer of household chores, an object of beauty and a source of pleasure, and put on a pedestal that soon resembles a cage.

Women have had to fight and fight hard to be able to vote, to be allowed to attend schools, to work outside the home and in decent conditions, to be paid a fair (but rarely equal) wage, and to be in sole possession of their own fortunes, personal and financial.

What we call the modern world is, for you as a woman, largely a product of that fight. It is a fight that is not completely won, but society is a much-improved place. In the United States, many of the obstacles that faced previous generations of women are gone. In other countries, the rights and privileges of women still vary considerably. Wherever you live, know that today, at this moment, so much is yours for the taking.

It is imperative that you discover, embrace, and honor the past work of heroic women by making the most of your life. It is imperative that you get an education, first and foremost. Don't squander this gift.

Remember this: the scariest thing in the world for some men is a woman with her own mind and her own money. That's exactly what you want to be. Education is the quickest way to get, and keep, both.

Wall Street or Main Street—The Big Benefits of Education

Whether you're going to work at a brokerage firm on Wall Street or a hardware store on Main Street, an education is going to serve you well throughout your life. So, if there's any way possible, take the opportunity to be a student if you can, when you can, where you can.

Wouldn't your life be richer if you exposed yourself to just a small part of the knowledge that has been articulated, preserved, and handed down over the past few thousand years? Consider and digest the wisdom of the ages. Marvel at the latest technological developments, innovations, and inventions that so often burst forth on college campuses. How could you change your life and world if you had the chance to build your skill set for employment and entrepreneurial opportunities? How might you enhance your understanding of current events if you had the chance to learn about history from a different, more nuanced perspective?

Study the mechanics of politics and money in order to make sure you aren't manipulated or victimized. Expand your mind. Deepen your understanding. Broaden your horizons.

Take advantage of what I call the *Big Benefits of Education.*

- *Big Benefit Number 1*: Knowledge for Its Own Sake. This enriches your life as you explore math, science, literature, art, politics, and history. You may not be an actor, but reading and appreciating Shakespeare or contemplating Rumi will deepen your understanding of the world.
- *Big Benefit Number 2*: Better Quality of Life. (Notice I didn't say 'standard of living'.) Quality of life requires a sufficient income to meet your material needs, but also includes an understanding of how best to manage your career, business and investment opportunities, personal life, financial assets, and leisure. You can make a great deal of money, but without an

education to learn how to manage and enjoy your wealth, you may have a very low quality of life.

- *Big Benefit Number 3*: Maximizing Opportunities. Give yourself the ability to identify and act upon opportunities to make this world a better place to live, for you and other people, for generations to come. This means volunteering, giving to charity, or going into public service. If you don't get a sufficient education or a quality education, you may spend all of your time and all of your energy simply surviving. You can't help anyone else if you can barely take care of yourself. And you can't really understand and address problems that affect others if you're unable to digest information and see things in context.
- *Big Benefit Number 4*: Creating Generational Wealth. Increase your ability to leave something to your children or to the world in the form of an inheritance or a legacy. Leaving a legacy gives other people more than money: it offers them options. That can be life-changing for them, and emotionally rewarding for you. You can facilitate social change. You can leave your mark. Consider the impact that Warren Buffet, Bill and Melinda Gates, and Jimmy and Rosalynn Carter have had on the world. Follow their lead.

You may be artistically or technically inclined. That's fine. I still encourage you to seek out a college education. Here are some of the differences a college education can make in your life:

- College graduates have more income earning potential;
- College graduates have more options in their careers;
- College graduates are less likely to divorce;
- College graduates enjoy better health;
- College graduates live longer.

Once again: the college experience is invaluable. Often, you enroll as an insecure teenager with no idea about the world. More often than not, you graduate as a young adult with a certain amount of perspective, knowledge, and skills under your belt to face the world with a degree of confidence and competence. Hopefully, you will also possess a heightened awareness of what is expected of you as a global citizen.

The Challenges and The Rewards

The challenges in getting an education are many. On the financial front there is the expense of tuition and often room and board. Student debt is daunting, even for middle-class families. If you have to work part-time or full-time, you'll need the commitment and discipline to push through early mornings at class and late nights at the job.

You'll need to look past friends your age who have 'good jobs' and spending money right now. You'll need to hold focus on your goals and postpone gratification. You'll need to ignore those in the media who tell you a college education may not be worth the effort and expense. Remember, most of these articles are written by pundits who *have* a college education and are published by executives *with* a college education.

The truth is that as you pursue and obtain an education, you will have set a worthwhile goal and accomplished it, which is key for your self-esteem. You will have something that cannot be taken away. It will last a lifetime. Its effects will bleed into every aspect of your life and nourish you in ways you can't imagine.

You will have documented certification of a certain level of competence and understanding. If your career path requires technical expertise, you will have verifiable proof of possessing that expertise. You will have a network of alumni to draw upon as you go forward into the workplace. You will be qualified for many more jobs, even if your field of study does not apply directly to your work.

Again, you will have entered an institution of higher learning as a teenager, with limited understanding, and graduated as a young adult, full of promise. You will be more empathetic, more mature, more prepared. These are just a few of the rewards of getting an education. If you did not have the opportunity to get an education immediately after high school, fear not. You can go to school or go back to school at any age. You can take classes online. You can take classes at night.

There is an abundance of resources to help you get an education. People of all ages, all over the world, know the value of an education and desperately want to learn.

A world of support and assistance is waiting. Loans and grants are available. Online courses are constantly on offer. Professional guidance about where and how to start, continue, or finish your education is there for anyone who wants it.

A word of caution about for-profit colleges: research their programs, prices, and promises carefully before putting your future in the hands of a company that is in business to make money. Private, state, and community colleges are your most reliable sources for getting the education, qualifications, and skills you need to succeed.

Business owners and public officials support and believe in education because there is a constant need for skilled workers and a preference for an educated populace. One ensures a society's prosperity. The other ensures its democracy. Each student's reasons are their own, but the blessings of education are universal: a better you, a better family, a better world.

Education and The Old Money Gal

Education is *the* priority for Old Money families. They set aside money for education first, before they make any other purchases or commitments. They may live in ramshackle houses, drive old cars, and favor well-worn clothes, but their children and grandchildren get a good education.

For the Old Money Gal, there is never really a question of whether or not she will get an education. Her parents and probably her grandparents have attended college. It's a family tradition. The Old Money Gal doesn't really decide if she's going to attend college: it's already been decided for her. She attends a very good public school or a private school as a child, then migrates into a prep school for four years before attending college. Her parents probably have a room in the house that is full of books, whether it's technically a library or not is unimportant: she is exposed to books and is expected to read. For the Old Money Gal, it's a book, not a big screen. It's a reading list, not a playlist.

If a specific area of interest develops in high school, she begins to work as an intern in the field during the summer to get a taste for the profession and to meet people. This practice continues in summers during college. In high school and college, she travels with her classmates and teachers, her family, and independently, as this is a key element of education. She may study abroad for a semester or a year in college. She most likely picks up a second language, usually French, which, by the way, is spoken by over 275 million people in the world, from Haiti to Quebec, Africa to Aix en Provence.

She understands the value of education lies not just in memorizing facts, but in learning to think critically; not just in getting a diploma to be qualified for a job, but in being exposed to ideas, past and present, that can enrich her future.

After she graduates from college, she continues to read, attend lectures and seminars, and take classes here and there. These experiences continually expose her to new ideas and new people, even if she works at the same job for several years. This fresh flow of information keeps her interested…and interesting.

~ OLD MONEY SECRET ~

> Education is the priority, the solid, time-tested path that, if taken, ensures quality of life. It is a cornerstone in the development of well-rounded, self-sufficient individuals. It is key to the acquisition and preservation of wealth, and, more importantly, the understanding of life.

* * * * * * * *

THINGS TO REMEMBER

Education is a lifetime endeavor. It doesn't end when you graduate from high school or when you graduate from college. Your best habit is constant education.

You can educate yourself by continuously and consistently reading worthwhile books. Read *A Tale of Two Cities* by Charles Dickens, then take in F. Scott Fitzgerald's *The Great Gatsby*. Pick up a biography on one of our Exemplars. Read Michel de Montaigne's *Essays* and compare those to Marcus Aurelius' *Meditations*.

Learn a new language. A new language is a second world. There are free online courses and videos, and probably people in your neighborhood who'll be delighted to help you learn. Pick up a new skill, whether it's a leisure activity that will enrich your weekends or vocational expertise that will *add value to you* in the workplace.

Perhaps the most important result of your education will be your ability to more effectively honor your commitments. Old Money Gal Maria Shriver learned this lesson from her grandmother, Rose Kennedy, when Ms. Shriver was attending college. Calling from a foreign country where she was enduring an unpleasant internship in less-than-posh conditions, Ms. Shriver complained to the Kennedy family matriarch and told her she wanted to cut the adventure short and come home. Mrs. Kennedy stopped her cold: 'Those people are counting on you. Honor your commitment.' And that was that.

The difference between you today and you ten years from now is the books you read and the people you meet. Read worthwhile books. Learn from skilled and experienced teachers, inside the classroom and out.

Prioritize education.

Note: as you think about the advantageous situation of an Old Money Gal, remember that someone in her family thought of her future years ago. They took action—through prioritizing, planning, and hard work—to make her education a reality. If you didn't have the same opportunity, you may be able to provide an education to someone else. There is no greater gift.

Exemplar – Simone Veil

Do you know Simone Veil? She was a French lawyer and politician who served as Minister of Health under Valéry Giscard d'Estaing, then as President of the European Parliament, and also as a member of the Constitutional Council of France.

A survivor of the Auschwitz-Birkenau concentration camp where she lost part of her family during the Holocaust, she served as the first president of the Fondation pour la Mémoire de la Shoah, from 2000 to 2007, and subsequently as honorary president.

After graduating from Institut d'études politiques de Paris with a law degree, Madame Veil spent several years practicing law. In 1956, she passed the national examination to become a magistrate. Holding a senior position at the National Penitentiary Administration under the Ministry of Justice, she was responsible for judicial affairs and improved women's prison conditions and the treatment of incarcerated women.

In 1964, she left to become the director of civil affairs, where she improved French women's general rights and status. She successfully achieved the right to dual parental control of family legal matters and adoptive rights for women. Advocating tirelessly for women's rights, she was best known for championing passage of the 1975 law which legalized a French woman's right to choose.

"French women never had a better friend," said one woman I stood next to as we watched Simone Veil's interment ceremony on July 1, 2018, at the Pantheon in Paris. Quite true, quite true.

If you're considering a life of public service, read more about Madame Simone Veil.

"Pain is the root of knowledge."

–Simone Veil

"Sell your cleverness and purchase bewilderment."

—Rumi

CHAPTER 4

The Goal Standard

Direction can be defined as the path that leads to a desired destination. That destination can include an ideal situation, an educational achievement, a profession, or a financial accomplishment.

You, as a woman, have never had greater freedom than you do today to choose the direction you want to take in life. You know this intellectually, but now is the time to embrace it emotionally and let it become personally true for you. To be truly happy, you want to take full responsibility for your success, to determine which direction you will travel in, and to make the important decisions about your life independently.

As you look at defining a direction in which you want your life to go, it might help to break things down into questions or categories, which you can ask yourself, make a list of the answers, then think about.

What seems like a 'big decision' might actually be a series of 'small choices'. The only caveat in this process is that you be completely honest with yourself as you ask the following:

- What do I want to be? i.e., a doctor, a lawyer, a novelist, a master sommelier, chess champion, or physicist;
- What do I want to do? i.e., bring healthcare to underprivileged children, reform campaign finance law, set up micro-finance banks in developing countries;
- What do I want to accomplish? i.e., be financially independent by the age of 40, open a library in my neighborhood, become a polyglot;
- What do I want to experience? i.e., travel, opera, a pilgrimage to India;
- What meaning and purpose is my life going to have? i.e., to teach, to employ people, to protect the environment, to make great films; and
- What impact will my work have on my loved ones, my community, and my world? i.e., a family trust to ensure the independence of future gen-

> erations, a scholarship fund for underprivileged children, a city park, a charity perpetually funded by royalties and licensing fees from intellectual properties that I acquire and own.

It is vitally important that, if possible, you do the work in life that you are truly passionate about, what you feel like you were put on this earth to do. If that's not possible right now, do the work you have to do—to the best of your ability—as you move toward the work you love to do.

Your Tool Kit

There's a universe of information on the topics of finding a direction and developing tools to be successful. Psychologists have written books and developed step-by-step exercises and tests to help you determine what you're good at and what you're interested in. Look to career counselors in school or in the private sector who can assist you in determining the best career or profession. Take full advantage of these resources if you aren't certain about the direction you want to take.

Look for information on the internet, but be selective. Motivational speakers and armchair philosophers (feel free to lump me into the latter category) clutter your local bookstore shelves as well as your Amazon and YouTube search results with books, strategies, seminars, and Top Ten Things You Need To Do So You Can…(Whatever). It's vitally important that you investigate these and learn about goal-setting, visualization, meditation, vision boards, and any practical tools that can help you find your direction and excel.

Remember: these techniques, strategies, and philosophies are tools; they are not ends in themselves. You take them and use them, like a can opener or a hammer, to become the person you want to be and get to the things you want in life. These involve listening, watching, or reading about concepts. These concepts can help you identify things in your personal life that you can change to get better results from life.

The tools that are truly valid always involve work and should not cost a great deal of money to implement. Books and online videos can be very helpful, and they usually don't cost you more than a pizza or a few minutes of your time. Additional resources are available at many universities' websites where you'll find free courses about every subject under the sun.

Effort

Once you've identified the tools and resources available to help you go in the direction you want to go, the next part of the equation is effort. Effort is defined as the action or work you put in a focused and disciplined manner in order to achieve a certain outcome. Once you decide on your direction, you then make an effort in that direction. You make this effort consistently, even if it means modifying current behavior (like sleeping late.) Modifying behavior over time is the way to make permanent changes happen. Effort is a *muscle.* It takes time to *build.* You must work to sustain it. Do the work. See the results. Remember: the idea of being an 'overnight success' is a myth.

The key phrase in the previous paragraph is 'over time'. This means, most often, that you *create new habits and/or change old habits* in order to improve your life. This is the unglamorous truth about being a better person and experiencing a higher quality of life.

As an example, I offer this challenge to you: when you wake up and get out of bed each morning, sit cross-legged on the floor, close your eyes, and remain still and silent for ten minutes. You can meditate, or you can vegetate, it matters not. The important thing is that you give yourself ten minutes to simply be aware. Do this simple thing every morning for 30 days, without interruption for weekends, holidays, or days you just don't feel like it.

Accepting this challenge will make you realize how difficult it can be to form a life-changing habit, even if it's as simple as sitting on the floor and being quiet and still for ten minutes. Forming a new habit usually requires 30 consecutive days of repeated behavior. If you can master yourself—and do what needs to be done, when it needs to be done, whether you like it or not—you can accomplish almost anything.

It's best to start small, with a simple, tangible thing like quiet time, and set a goal for 30 days. Address one thing at a time, until that thing becomes a habit. Then move on to the next thing you want to change, the next habit you want to form.

Emotion

The common danger that most people encounter when they decide to change their life is that they become too emotional about a self-improvement program. They set unrealistic goals, like losing a pound a day over 30 days. Then obstacles, setbacks, or lackluster results appear. Discouraged and frustrated, they quickly give up on their objective, return to previous behavior patterns, and live the same life.

Often this happens because people aren't honest with themselves about their own capabilities. The other issue may be that they're vulnerable to the too-good-to-be-true promises made on infomercials and YouTube videos, i.e., "You'll be the next no-money-down real estate millionaire." Not everyone is meant to be a real estate millionaire, an internet billionaire, best-selling author, or a pop icon. There are entire industries that prosper in America by preying upon people's illusions about themselves and their abilities. (Feel free not to lump me in with those.)

Emotions are a key part of life, but to improve, we need to harness new habits to those emotions and follow through with purpose. This requires resolve, which is an emotion, but not the same thing as 'emotion'. Resolve is an emotion with a purpose and a plan attached to it.

As an example, let's look at a woman who is overweight. She has tried different diets and different exercise programs, but she can't seem to discipline herself consistently to make them work and see results. Finally, she has a heart-to-heart conversation with a girlfriend. She admits her failures, and shares her frustration with her close friend. Her friend is sympathetic, but senses the underlying issue.

'If you keep going the way you're going, you're going to have serious health problems,' her friend says bluntly. 'I know', admits the woman. 'Heart disease. Diabetes.'

'And your kids? What's going to happen to them if you're not healthy enough to take care of them? Take them to ballgames and concerts? What if you're not even around at all to see them grow up?'

That question resonates with the woman. It is an emotional issue deep enough and important enough to create resolve. The woman realizes how important her health is, not just to herself, but to her family. She decides to work consistently and gradually to exercise regularly and eat better. She sets goals to lose weight. She shares these goals with her husband and kids, so, when they see her making good choices about food and activities, they support and encourage her. She gathers information thoroughly, assembles and organizes her tools, and makes the maximum, consistent effort. This combination ensures optimal results.

~ OLD MONEY SECRET ~

> Life is most fully lived with a direction, a purpose. This purpose is beyond the sedentary enjoyment of leisure and the simple acquisition of wealth. Direction must have meaning and enduring value. Each person must decide on their own what direction their life will take.

* * * * * * * *

THINGS TO REMEMBER

You want to *have* a direction and also *define it in detail.* Create vivid, three-dimensional goals and dreams about what you want to be and do. Look at yourself in an honest—but not limited—light. To help you define your direction, let's again inquire within... Ask yourself:

- What do I really enjoying doing?
- What am I naturally good at?
- With my skill set, interests, and personality, where do I fit in?
- What credentials or experience do I need to obtain in order to be qualified to do what I really love?
- Am I willing to work to get those credentials or experience, intensely and consistently?
- If not, why not?
- What industry, field, or profession do I naturally gravitate toward?
- Do I feel like the people working in that industry are 'kindred spirits'?

- What kind of plan can I put together, with step-by-step actions, tangible targets, and reasonable deadlines, to move in the direction of doing what I want to do?
- What resources are available to me that can help me get there?

Remember: you may envision yourself, teaching a classroom full of students, working at a national park, or doing research in a lab. When you have an image in your mind, and you feel excited, make a mental note of that: you may have discovered your direction.

Exemplar – Edith Wharton

Born to privilege, Edith Wharton was also born to write, and write she did. She published her first poem at the age of 15, authored more than 85 short stories and 15 novels, and, in 1921, was the first woman to win a Pulitzer Prize for Literature.

A child of the Civil War, she was three years old when the Confederate States surrendered. After the war, her family traveled extensively in Europe enabling her to become fluent in French, German, and Italian. She rejected the standards of fashion and etiquette that were expected of young girls at the time, considering these fashions superficial and oppressive. Ms. Wharton also wanted more education than she received, so she read voraciously from her father's library and borrowed—sometimes without permission—from the libraries of her father's friends.

On vacation in Paris when World War I broke out, Ms. Wharton didn't flee to safety like most everyone else. She stayed and offered assistance to unemployed French women and refugees, held fundraisers for the war effort, and opened tuberculosis hospitals. She was made a Chevalier of the Legion of Honor by the French president for her efforts. It wasn't because she played it safe. If you have a passion for writing, read about the life of Edith Wharton.

"There are two ways of spreading light:
to be the candle, or the mirror that receives it."

—Edith Wharton

"Be fiercely independent of the good opinions of others."

—Abraham H. Maslow

CHAPTER 5

Under The Influence

Another question to ask yourself regarding direction is this: 'Who makes the decision about which direction I go in?' Answer: 'I do.' You are the captain of your ship. '*I make my own decisions.*' If you are a single adult woman, this is your mantra. You may still be dependent upon your parents to some extent. You may be in a relationship with another person, participating and sharing in the decision-making process.

The truth of the matter, however, is that unless you are a guest of your state or federal authorities (in prison, that is), you can and should make your own decisions about the important things in your life. The danger is that you may think you already do, and this may not be the whole truth.

There are three major *influences* you may be under that may negatively impact your ability to make good decisions and choose your own direction in life. They are:

- mass media;
- friends; and
- family.

We'll look at each of these in detail in an attempt to manage and reduce their impact on your life.

The Influence of the Media

Let's discuss mass media first. If you watch four or five hours of television a day, you're probably not making your own decisions about the food you eat, the beauty products you use, or the clothes you wear. You're watching commercials and television programs that *influence* you to a huge degree and begin to make choices for you.

Companies spend billions of dollars on advertising for a reason: it works. It shapes people's decision-making process, making them purchase things they don't really need and even things that are not really good for them. It also contributes to a huge transfer of wealth from consumers to corporations, to the benefit of the latter at the expense of the former. A tremendous amount of research, deliberation, and effort goes into the work of separating you from your hard-earned money. Often, retailers are persuading you to purchase things that are not necessities.

For example, you don't need a $50,000 car. However, when you repeatedly watch smart, slick car commercials filled with happy actors driving down the California coastline, with the sunroof open, the music playing, laughing all the way...you slowly begin to believe that you do need a $50,000 car.

You don't need a $45.00 lipstick. Then, you see that beautiful model in the magazine ad or on the billboard wearing the same lipstick and she looks sultry, sexy, skinny, and confident. You want to be sultry, sexy, skinny, and confident. You don't think the ad has any effect on you, but then, despite not being able to afford it, you find yourself walking by the cosmetics counter at the department store. You see—oh my!—the $45.00 lipstick! Then, you find yourself buying the $45.00 lipstick. Or, worse yet, having a drawer full of unused $45.00 lipsticks in every color under the sun. *Come on, ladies.*

Warning: this is the power of the mass media. You don't need all these things, but advertising makes you think you do. Revelation: the time and money you spend browsing for and purchasing frivolous consumer products is better spent on purchasing your freedom through education, exercise, and self-improvement. Know their game. Stay on your game.

Many people find themselves overweight, seriously ill, or in debt because of this powerful undue influence that negatively impacts their lives. The fact that people spend billions of dollars a year on soft drinks which contribute to a variety of illnesses is just one obvious example. More specifically, have you ever noticed that a certain product is not good for you and that you really don't need it? Nonetheless, you can't resist the impulse to purchase it? (One more lipstick...that soft drink... or those shoes). *It's not good for you, you don't need it, but you still buy it.* This illogical sequence of events is symptomatic of someone who's been subtly brainwashed by advertising.

Advertising is not the only culprit. The internet is fertile ground for corporations and governments to get into your head and shape your opinions. Its evil spawn, social media, can warp your perspective, corrupt your priorities, and expose you to undue influence from often anonymous sources with hidden agendas.

In order to clear your mind of undue influence, it can be helpful to reduce your exposure to mass media, namely television, radio, and the internet. Obviously, the internet is a great source for information and a great platform for communication. Use it wisely.

One Step Back

There are steps you can take to minimize the influence of the internet and social media on your life. Limit your Daily Internet Exposure (DIE) to an hour a day outside work. Shift your social interactions from digital to real time: a cup of coffee with a friend instead of a text; a dinner with real-world friends instead of a post to Facebook friends; take a walk in the park instead of watching endless YouTube videos.

Pull back from media influence as a first step toward making decisions for yourself. Avoid 'feel good' purchases, 'impulse' shopping, and 'power' purchases, i.e., purchases made that give you a feeling of power or control. The fact that you can buy something doesn't mean you have power. It just means you've made a choice to spend money.

'BOGO' (buy one get one free) is an effective marketing strategy. Be aware of it and avoid it. Avoid the 'just in case' purchases as well. The 'just in case' purchase is often a rationale to spend money on something that may or may not be used for an event or situation which may or may not occur in the near or distant future. Don't kid yourself: you're wasting money. Purchase things when you need them. Ask yourself if you're guilty of any of the following:

- wearing the clothes and makeup the media tells you to buy, looking a lot like everybody else, and maybe spending more money than you should;
- carrying the purse you've seen advertised in fashion magazines because it provides you with a sense of status, even if you're working for minimum wage;

- driving a car you've seen advertised on television, because on television *everyone is having so damn much fun driving that car! And it's so cute! Oh my god!*

Again, media influence can be costly. How many people do you know who have drawers full of cosmetics and beauty products they never use? Or exercise equipment that does nothing more than sit in the garage or act as a clothes hanger in the spare bedroom? Or pay monthly rent on personal storage units to hold unused, surplus household items that they never use?

These examples are the results of excessive consumer spending. Below are some symptoms consumers exhibit when they've been unduly influenced by advertising. Which if any of these statements true for you?

- I purchase things I don't need;
- I don't understand why I make these purchases;
- I have difficulty not purchasing things;
- I walk around a mall or department store in a zombie-like stupor, looking aimlessly for something to purchase;
- I feel a sense of personal accomplishment or euphoria when I make a purchase;
- I don't use the items that I purchase;
- I'm in debt or broke because of my spending.

Let me share some wisdom from a friend of mine. She's a well-educated, affluent, and charming young lady who lives in New York City. She has a fulfilling career and a circle of great friends. She dresses elegantly, stylishly, and simply.

We met in a hotel lobby around Christmas time. I asked her if she'd been shopping. She shook her head dismissively, and added that she shops about four days a year. The rest of her time is spent working, traveling, socializing, mentoring, and reading. She lifted her tea cup to her lips, and then almost whispered to me, *'The more cluttered the closet, the emptier the life.'*

Note: keep your life uncluttered. Guard your mind and your quiet time, day in and day out, so you can determine the best direction for you, long term and short term. Be aware of what you read. Take care of who and what you listen to on television and on the internet. Make sure you're really making your own decisions and going in your own direction, without undue influence. And, as a great Indian poet once said, be suspicious of what you want.

Why is this issue of negative media influence so vitally important? Because every dollar you're spending on stuff is a dollar you're not investing in you. Focus and invest in intellectual or educational pursuits. Avoid distracting consumer pursuits. Your money follows your focus: set your priorities yourself. Go your own way.

The Influence of Friends

To make sure you're the one primarily in control of the direction your life is taking, it's often necessary to take an objective inventory of your friends. Your friends know you, intimately. They've been around you for a long time, so they're important to you. They can be a great source of encouragement and support as you pursue your goals and share life experiences. They can be a source of great comfort and support for you in difficult times, and you can do the same for them.

Likewise, they can sometimes persuade you to do less-than-brilliant things you would never otherwise do. Peer pressure is a very real thing, and sometimes not a good thing. You have so much in common that you may think choices that make sense for them also make sense for you. This may not always be so.

It is a time-tested fact that you will become like your friends. Don't think you are different in this regard. You will adopt many of their attitudes and habits over time. If your aspirations differ markedly from theirs, your friendships will likely fade.

You will either study harder or study less depending upon your friends. You'll either get into trouble or get into grad school depending on your friends. You'll either save or waste money depending on your friends. And when you're successful, you'll either have to watch your back or enjoy a pat on the back, depending upon your friends.

You may be able to have a beer or a cup of coffee every once in a while with your friends who have taken a different road than you, but you won't be able to spend quality time and really share important things with them. If you're saving and planning to start a new business and they're raising hell at the local pub every night, don't expect much camaraderie, support, or understanding. They don't have the same priorities as you. They may not be going in the same direction or share your values anymore.

Key things to ask yourself right now about your friends, collectively and individually, include the following:

- Can I rely on them?
- Can they rely on me?
- Do they encourage me to do the right thing?
- Do I feel better after spending time with them?
- Do they have constructive goals for their own lives?
- Do they send a card on my birthday? Do I do that for them?
- Do they let me know about it if I've behaved inappropriately?
- Do they make a sincere effort to keep in touch throughout the year?
- Even if our ambitions differ, is everyone supportive of everyone else?
- Do they ask me for money or expect me to pay all the time when we're out together?
- Do they let me know if they think I may be in danger or may be making a really big, bad decision?
- Are they there for me—meaning do they show up and offer emotional support—when something good or bad happens to me?

A rule for you, and for your friends: if it's not nice, don't do it. If it's not true, don't say it.

Embrace and nurture the friendships that are up-lifting. Moderate the time and energy you spend with those who are constantly complaining and gossiping. Retreat from toxic individuals who look to sabotage your efforts to be happy and get ahead.

'Up your game' in being a good friend to those you care about. Make the extra effort to keep in touch. Remember birthdays. Buy and give gifts on time. Send cards. Take the initiative and coordinate events for your friends to get together for no reason other than to get together.

Remember: in order to chart your own course in life, you're going to have to determine if your friends are supportive or holding you back, intentionally or not. This is your life. Value it. Friends are worth their weight in gold. Cherish them.

The Influence of Family

The most deep-seated and difficult directional influence to recognize is often the influence of your family. Because you have spent, many times, all of your young life around them, their influence may be too great, too overpowering, too invasive. This influence may not take into consideration that you are your own person with your own educational and professional goals. This all-encompassing influence may affect your ability to objectively choose your direction in life. Your immediate family—parents and siblings—are usually the most influential. Grandparents—unless they became your 'parents' and raised you—aunts, uncles, and cousins have less influence most of the time.

The first fact that can contribute to their less-than-healthy influence is that you came into your family as a baby. You've probably spent your childhood years in the care of your family. They most likely still see you as a child, even if you're 35 years old with a career and children of your own.

The second part of the problem is that they love you, they think they know you well, and they think they know what's best for you. It's difficult for your family—especially your immediate family members—to not project their own fears, limitations, hopes, and dreams onto your life. Don't blame them: they're human. The challenge with family is that it's an emotional mixed bag: you have positive feelings and negative feelings for the same people, often to the extreme in both instances.

In fairness, it's important to acknowledge the positive influence than your family has probably had on you. If it's a positive influence, you want to confirm it, be grateful for it, and use it to fuel your endeavors. In most families, there's a wealth of knowledge, experience, support, and expertise. If possible, take advantage of those. Listen to your family members. Learn from them. Sift through their stories and advice for pearls of wisdom that can be of value to you.

Much of what you have learned and much of the influence your family has over you may be constructive. If you're lucky, they told you that you're special, that you're intelligent, that you have potential. They supported your efforts to be a good student, to be a good person. They taught you not to lie, cheat, or steal. They scolded you when you tried to kill your little brother, even if he deserved it. They respected your opinions and choices even when they disagreed with them.

A good exercise is to make a list of what your parents and family have done for you that you appreciate. It may be as simple as feeding you and clothing you from birth to age 18. It may be as expansive as giving you a college education and the resources to travel around the world. Most likely, the very fundamentals of it are that your parents loved you, raised you, and want the best for you, in spite of their faults. Make the list. Write it down, and the next time you're visiting with them, read the list to them, expressing your gratitude for what they did as parents. Do this in person. Don't criticize anything. Don't qualify anything. Just express your appreciation.

If your family has had an overall positive and constructive impact on your life, you have to honor that. Make the time and effort to see them. Spend quality time together. They were there for you. Be there for them.

Remember: if you encounter something in life that is positive, you want to confirm it, be grateful for it, and use it to fuel your endeavors. If it's a negative, you want to articulate it, isolate it, and distance it from your definition of who you are.

Speaking of the negative...Your parents may have said and done things that may not have been helpful, and even hurtful and harmful. They may have said or implied that you're not that smart, that your abilities are limited, that you're not a person someone else could ever love. They may have sabotaged your efforts to progress by threatening to withdraw their love if you move on, or laid guilt on you for wanting more or being different. They may also disapprove of your decisions, as they are not the decisions they would have made. Don't feel like you're alone here.

Break these memories and feelings down into smaller, more manageable elements. First, look at your parents' intentions toward you as a child, and then look at their intentions toward you as an adult. Have these intentions evolved as you've become an adult? Or do they still treat you like a child? Whatever your answers are to these two questions, simply repeat to yourself: 'I make my own decisions.'

Recognize that a painful, negative influence by a family member is not always a verbal statement made in the open. It can be subtle, manipulative behavior, which is worse because you can't as easily identify it and address it. This type of influence and behavior may color your self-image and may negatively impact your self-worth. It can hinder personal growth and breed resentment.

If you feel your family has an overall negative impact on your life, there are three things you can do: *make your own money, live your own life, and live it at a distance.* If you can't move to a different city, put up your own boundaries. If you can't support yourself, get a second job. Be attentive about what information you share and who you share it with. Be attentive about being too available for needy family members. Moderate your responses to your family's behavior. Maintain your integrity. Don't be self-destructive or contrary just to make a point.

Understand that sometimes your family is meddling in your affairs, and sometimes they are expressing genuine concern. Try to recognize the difference. Do this by considering the source and the intent. Ask yourself: is this a typical concern for a mother or father? Then ask yourself: what are they trying to accomplish with this behavior? Is it to control me? Keep me safe? Help me in the long run? Hold me back?

If you're in eminent physical danger, a victim of domestic violence, addicted to alcohol or drugs, or risking the health and safety of your own children, then your parents have a right to get into your personal business and, with the assistance of qualified professionals, intervene. Otherwise, they get to leave you in peace.

Keep in touch regularly, but not frequently. Share information selectively. 'Let them read about in the newspapers,' is how one Old Money Gal put it when asked if she was going to tell her parents she'd sold her company. I'm guessing they had some issues, but she had definitely come to terms with who she needed approval or recognition from, and it wasn't Mom and Dad.

Old Money, Independent Thinking

'Am I rich? Yes.
I can afford to think for myself.'

—an OMG

Being inner-directed is a marked characteristic of an Old Money Gal. So many of them simply do not give a damn about what you, I, or anybody else thinks. *Of course,* you say, *she's independently wealthy and doesn't have to worry about getting or keeping a job. She can afford to be oblivious to the opinions of others. She can drive an old car, dress like an old lady, and say anything she wants.*

I would humbly suggest that you back-burner the financial aspect of an Old Money Gal's free-thinking attitude and consider other factors.

- First, she was most likely raised in a family devoid of cliche status symbols, i.e. things that are purchased and displayed to impress other people. Life, as she learned it, was not about impressing other people;

- Second, she was educated at school and at home about how to behave, regardless of how others behave. That is to say, politely, with integrity, but also with sometimes brutal honesty. So a certain objectivity and autonomy were instilled at a young age;

- Third, she was encouraged to seek a profession and create a life that suits *her*, not the expectations of others. (Sometimes, however, a family business does exact a limit on the options some descendants have. Duty is a real thing.)

From this perspective, financial independence is only a small factor when it comes to an Old Money Gal choosing, shaping, and creating a life. She would most likely live it, with or without money, because the key elements of it—doing what you love for a living, marrying whoever you want, and going your own way—aren't really dependent upon money.

THINGS TO REMEMBER

Everybody wants to make more money; only a few are willing to make more of themselves first.

It's often helpful to have a role model. Find someone who is doing the work you want to do. Use the internet wisely: find out how they got where they are. How did they start? Can you follow their path? Can you model their behavior? Are the resources they used available to you?

Carve out some time each week to enjoy a hobby or passion that is completely fulfilling on its own, independent of your future goals. This will breathe joy into your life as you move forward and add a little padding to the sometimes bumpy road of finding your direction and improving yourself overall.

As you consider professional options, be honest about the career you say you want, the work you're really willing to do, and the sacrifices you're truly willing to make. Be just as honest about the relationships you say you want and the effort you're willing to commit to in order to make them shine.

Listen to other people, especially (and only) people who know you well and wish you well. Review your natural inclinations and your childhood dreams. Ask yourself: if money was not a concern, if what other people thought was not a concern, what would you want to be and do?

In journalism, reporters are advised to get the 'who, what, where, when' (and maybe how) of something in order to write a story about it. If the story is 'Your Life', let's look at these and apply them, even if they don't fall into that exact order:

- *Where* are you going? If you articulate the direction you want to go in, it's then fairly simple to get a 'laundry list' of the things that will be required to go in that direction and accomplish that goal, whether it's a professional or financial goal, or a personal, spiritual one.

- *What* are your priorities? Once you—and you alone—have decided on your direction, your priorities will fall into place. They must match up with your direction or goal. For example, if your goal is to be a doctor, your priority will be studying, not partying. Be steadfast in your priorities.

- *How* can you get where you want to go or become what you want to be? When there's a will, there's a way. Make your plans. Chart your course. Be flexible in how you get there.

- *Who* can help you get there? Once you've made your plan, done your research, and started the work, look for teachers, mentors, partners, or employers to help you achieve your goals, refine your skills, or maximize your results.

- *When* are you taking action? There will be certain choices to make and certain 'things to do' at certain points in time. You can review your tent-poles for guidance on this.

You are constantly making decisions, big and small, whether you realize it or not, about the direction your life is taking. Become aware of this. Get good at it. First, say to yourself, 'I make decisions for me and my life.' Then ask yourself, 'What are my options?' Do your best to identify your options on your own. They may be unpleasant, but that's okay. Then ask others who you think, by experience, education, or intellect, are qualified to provide information you seek.

Ask questions. Take notes. Don't interrupt. The smart people will ask you questions, too, in order to get a clearer picture of where you are and where you want to go. The smart people will give you options to consider. Alarm bells should go off if someone tells you that you don't have any options. Seek information first, then opinions. Everybody has an opinion. Not everyone has relevant information.

If you live in Lubbock, Texas, and have a job offer from a major corporation in New York City, who are you going to ask for insight and advice about this decision? Someone who's lived in Lubbock their entire life and has never worked for a major corporation? Or someone who's worked for a major corporation in New York City? I'm not bashing Lubbock, of course. I'm encouraging you to seek out the best information available and relevant to you, i.e., information that is verifiable, that is based on evidence and experience. Consider someone's feelings about a subject last, if at all. Caveat: if ten people have had the same experience with something, and feel the same way about their experience, listen carefully, and ask more questions.

Who are you listening to? Are these people where you want to be? Do they have an agenda, individually or collectively, that shades their opinions? Ask yourself: Do they know me? Do they want the best for me? Do they have influence over me? (If you are aware of this and acknowledge this, you can moderate this.) Your intuition sometimes plays a part in making a good decision, but information will serve you well consistently.

Finding your direction and going in that direction with a minimum of outside interference is constant work. It takes asking hard questions, acknowledging inconvenient or unpleasant truths about yourself or your options, and tuning out undue influence. Sometimes, it's like eating rocks. Still, it's something that needs to be done if you're going to live life on your own terms and live it fully. Remember that. Do the work. Enjoy the rewards of embracing your own direction. Remember: be fiercely independent of the good opinion of others.

EXEMPLARS – JANE GOODALL & DELORES HUERTA

Bonus! Two Exemplars! Consider the lives of the scientist, Dr. Jane Goodall and activist Dolores Huerta.

First, Dr. Goodall. At the age of 26, Dr. Goodall's passion for primates compelled her to leave a comfortable Old Money life in Britain and move to the African jungle, where she lived in primitive conditions for years in order to study chimpanzees. Her discovery that chimpanzees make and use tools is considered one of the most important revelations of the 20th century. In 1977, she established the Jane Goodall Institute which advocates for the conservation of natural resources and open spaces.

In 2002, she was named a United Nations Messenger of Peace. Considered to be the world's foremost expert on chimpanzees, Dr. Goodall is best known for her over 55-year study of social and family interactions of wild chimpanzees in Gombe Stream National Park, Tanzania, which began in 1960.

Thanks to her advocacy, fewer animals are abused in laboratories and more enjoy a safe existence in the wild. Thanks to her research, we as humans see how much more we have in common with not just chimps, but all animals. Hopefully, her work will inspire each of us to be kinder.

If you love animals and think you may want to work with them, learn about the life and work of Dr. Jane Goodall.

"We have the choice to use the gift of our life to make the world a better place–or not to bother".

–Jane Goodall

Now, Delores Huerta. Absent the steadfast, difficult, and often dangerous work done by Delores Huerta, the United Farm Workers organization would probably not exist. She and Mr. Caesar Chavez founded the organization to fight for the rights of migrant workers and negotiate labor contracts for them in the 1960s. (Migrant workers are responsible for the harvesting of most of the food that ends up on your dining room table each night. Kind of demanding, essential work.)

She advocated for laws that allowed workers to take the California drivers license test in Spanish, and to ensure that federal child welfare programs were available to the children of migrant workers. Her efforts brought her national acclaim. They also brought physical danger: in 1968, she stood next to Robert Kennedy only minutes before he was assassinated at the Ambassador Hotel in Los Angeles. At a peaceful demonstration in 1968, she was severely beaten by members of the San Francisco Police Department. The incident was caught on videotape, and she subsequently received a large financial settlement from the city. In typical style, she used the proceeds to benefit farm workers, not herself.

If you feel your future lies in public service, investigate Delores Huerta's legacy.

"We as women should shine light on our accomplishments and not feel egotistical when we do. It's a way to let the world know that we as women can accomplish great things!"

–Dolores Huerta

"Be yourself, unapologetically."

—Kesha

CHAPTER 6

The Going Get Tough

The Extremely Challenging Endeavor (the 'ECE') is a physically, mentally, and emotionally difficult task or experience in which a person is isolated from a familiar environment and is forced to marshal their own resources in order to complete the given task. I encourage you to put yourself through at least one.

The purpose of this experience is to permanently change the person for the better. They become more competent, more disciplined, more self-reliant, and more confident.

If you haven't had the trauma/privilege of boarding school, or the formative experience of military service, seek out your own ECE. I don't recommend putting yourself in physical danger, but a physically demanding element to the ECE is often helpful.

Note: before you do anything physically demanding or risky, consult your physician. Prepare and train, get professional assistance. Use equipment that is in good condition. Be safe as you challenge yourself. An ECE may result in you having blisters on your feet. It should not result in your leg being in a cast.

You may want to hike the Appalachian Trail, run a marathon, climb a mountain, or bicycle across your state. The options are wide open. The only limits are what you can do physically and how much time you can take to do them. Investing in yourself is key. The ECE is going to do the following:

- Develop a results oriented, not appearances oriented, mindset;
- Enable you to put the opinions of others in their proper place, as 'others' are not going to be with you when you take on this challenge, endure these hardships, and discover new strengths and weaknesses about yourself;
- Exhaust you physically and challenge you mentally;
- Expand what you think you're capable of;

- Establish a foundation of personal confidence and resourcefulness which you can draw upon going forward, in all aspects of your life.

Some of you may be saying to me right now, 'You know, Byron, not to cut you off, but just getting out of my family situation/school/neighborhood was an Extremely Challenging Endeavor.' I completely understand that. I don't have a 'one size fits all' attitude about the advice I offer. You may now have street smarts and toughness that serve you well. Maybe you go on a more spiritual quest, like taking a vow of silence for a week (I'd suggest being on vacation from your job); going offline with your laptop and cell phone for a week; meditating every day for a month. It may be an educational pursuit: getting your MBA or a law degree, or learning computer programming while you're working full time.

Whatever your ECE is, when you're doing it, it needs to demand all of your attention and all of your effort. As an example, in 2017, my wife completed the Camino de Santiago, walking 629 miles across northern Spain in 28 days. (Photos of her adventure grace the pages of this book.) She trekked from Saint Jean Pied du Port in France, across the Pyrenees and into Spain. Sometimes alone, and sometimes in the company of other 'pilgrims' (as they're called), she hauled herself and her backpack through the countryside. Each day offered something new—pouring rain, enchanted forests, baking plains—and familiar comforts, most notably the generosity of the Spanish people who shared their food, accommodations, and prayers each step of the way. There was no time to care about hair, makeup, gossip, or small talk. What was *trending on the internet* mattered not. Familiar surroundings, distractions, and modern conveniences were gone. The environment was new and unknown. The focus was on the task at hand.

That task was, again, physically and emotionally challenging and results-oriented, i.e., getting up at dawn and walking 15 to 20 miles to the next town without delay, so she could eat, rest, wash her clothes, hang them to dry, plan the next leg of the journey, and go to bed early. She enjoyed the experience. But, then again, she attended Catholic school in Boston, so this wasn't her first ECE, if you know what I mean.

If you served in the armed forces, your boot camp was your ECE. If you didn't, then you must find your own personal ECE. It should strip off the petty insecurities we all carry around, force a mental toughness to set in, and let you exit the experience with a different, improved image of yourself based on your successful completion of the challenge.

The ECE is an investment in you. The endeavor itself is external, physical, and tangible, an accomplishment you can quantify: example, 'I hiked the Grand Canyon.' The change will be internal, psychological, and may be less obvious to others: a personal, private evolution you cannot easily articulate, i.e., the person you become when you've finished your ECE.

'Good steel can withstand any temperature.'

—Gabriel Betancourt

Old Money and the ECE

Old Money families introduce their offspring to an ECE when they send their obviously privileged and potentially spoiled daughter off to boarding school, often before the age of 16. The school is typically steeped in tradition. Its time-tested expertise lies in building character, instilling discipline, forging self-confidence, and developing intellectual rigor in its students.

The school will welcome this sheltered young lady, and her new classmates, and introduce them to a new world. She'll say goodbye to her parents. She'll bring her suitcases to her assigned room, with a roommate or several roommates. She'll be a freshman. She'll learn the school's written and unwritten rules, taking orders and advice from sophomore, junior, and senior year students.

She'll learn reading, writing, and arithmetic, to be sure. She'll study the classics, learn a foreign language, and participate in school-sponsored activities. She'll also juggle a busy schedule of classes, study time, sports, and theatre. Time management will be mastered. Mental focus will be required. Team spirit will blossom between her and her classmates. She'll learn to be organized, punctual, and polite. She'll also learn to be generous: there will certainly be classmates who need her help in one subject or during a difficult moment, just as much as she'll need theirs. Lifelong friendships will start here. She'll get up early, wear the same school uniform everyone else wears, eat with everyone else, and attend classes with everyone else.

Administrators will require her attendance in class. Teachers will demand that she listen, learn, participate, and study. Student tutors will work with her and encourage her until she thoroughly understands the concepts and information that are being taught. She will not be able to pull rank by dropping her family's name: most of her classmates come from wealthy families, and some of her European classmates may even be members of the nobility, aristocracy, or royalty. She will not be able to gain any traction with her looks: there are plenty of pretty girls here, and the mandatory uniforms instantly eliminate any 'fashion competition'. In short, none of these matter.

This ECE of boarding school will separate this uncertain child from her comfortable, loving family home and isolate her in an often harsh, demanding, results-oriented environment. She will be forced to dig in, find her way, take orders, stand up for herself, make her grades, and work and live with others. It's sometimes a rude awakening. It's often a family tradition. It always prepares her for adulthood.

During this process, she will learn to reason, to analyze, to focus, to compete, to be part of a team. The girl who could have easily turned into an unbearable, spoiled-rotten princess will become a self-reliant, confident, and educated young lady. When she graduates, the purpose of this ECE will have been fulfilled: to educate, to build character, to instill confidence, to find purpose, and to forge all of these, like sharp and strong steel, into a woman who's ready to face the world.

After a grueling four years at prep school, it's often off to an Ivy League school where the scholastic requirements are equally daunting. Of course, there is time for fun, both in boarding school and college, but the intellectual demands strip an Old Money child of any illusions of grandeur. Most importantly, this ECE shapes an identity based on her own efforts and accomplishments. It allows her to come into her own, with confidence to be her best self, unapologetically.

As one novelist so eloquently put it: prison is hard for those who haven't attended an English boarding school.

~ OLD MONEY SECRET ~

Old Money families invest in their children by ensuring they experience an ECE: an Extremely Challenging Endeavor. This can involve boarding school, military service, or sports. It forces the child to draw upon their own resources and forge an independent identity away from comfortable surroundings, away from privilege.

* * * * * * * *

EXEMPLAR – ELEANOR ROOSEVELT

As niece to one US President and wife to another, public service was second nature to Eleanor Roosevelt. A tireless advocate for women, minorities, and the working class, she is consistently listed as one of the most admired people of the 20th century. Among other accomplishments, she was the first chair of the United Nations Commission on Human Rights.

In 1921, Ms. Roosevelt began serving as a stand-in for her incapacitated husband, President Franklin Roosevelt, making public appearances on his behalf. She also worked with the Women's Trade Union League (WTUL), raising funds in support of the union's goals: a 48-hour work week, minimum wage, and the abolition of child labor. (We have much to thank her for.) The wife of a president who was elected to serve four times, she was the only First Lady many young Americans knew until her husband died in office.

When she entered the Oval Office the day after her husband's death, Harry Truman, Vice President and soon-to-be president, was meeting with advisors, struggling with the challenges the country faced in the midst of World War II.

He stood instantly and approached her. "Mrs. Roosevelt, what can we do for you?" he asked tenderly. She took his hand and replied, "Oh, no, Mr. Truman. What can we do for *you*?"

It doesn't get any classier than that.

> *"A woman is like a tea bag: you can't tell how strong she is until you put her in hot water."*
>
> —ELEANOR ROOSEVELT

"You must embrace pain and use it as fuel for your journey."

—Kenji Miyazawa

May 25, 2017—The Meseta, Burgos, Spain

CHAPTER 7

Decisions, Decisions

A 'protocol' may refer to an 'original document' from which subsequent documents or agreements are drawn. For our purposes, protocols will refer to preset rules and guidelines that govern behavior and frame choices. Protocols can be effectively used to maximize opportunities and happiness and minimize mistakes.

Many people (including me) often create a protocol only after a particularly unpleasant experience. "I'll never do that again," is one of the most common responses to a mistake. We've all heard someone else say it, and we've all said it ourselves. Whatever the oath pertains to, if it's honored, the behavior going forward is governed by that protocol. Hopefully, future results from the changed behavior are much improved, or at least the mistake is not repeated.

This is the hard and often costly value of experience. It's been said that if you learn something, you'll remember it; but if you experience something, you'll know it. Think of it as the difference between someone who watches a documentary about war on television and someone who's actually been to war.

To avoid an unpleasant experience, you can create protocols. These are rules that you create and live by, decisions you make in advance. The direction and quality of your life will be reflected in the protocols that you hold most dear. You may want to create protocols for the following categories:

The Spiritual

- how you interpret and 'live' your religion, philosophy, or spiritual practice;
- what rituals and traditions you observe (example: 'I meditate every morning.');
- what commitment you may or may not make to non-violence;
- how you translate your spiritual philosophy into daily interactions with other people.

The Personal

- how you conduct your daily affairs, i.e., making commitments (slowly), honoring them (always), and complaining about doing so (never);
- how you budget your time, your energy, and your generosity;
- how you commit to your emotional health on a regular basis;
- how you plan to exercise (example: 'I do yoga five days a week');
- what you eat and don't eat;
- what you drink and don't drink;
- what drugs you use and avoid;
- what you read and how often;
- how often you travel, to where, and for what purpose;
- how you honor your commitments to your spouse or partner;
- how you honor and provide for your children.

The Professional

- how you conduct yourself in the workplace with regard to your colleagues;
- how you conduct yourself in the workplace with regard to ethical or legal issues;
- how much time you intend to commit to work each day or week;
- how much time and money you intend to commit to improving your professional skills through continuing education or training;
- what professional title, certification, or position you plan to achieve (example: 'I'm going to be a pediatrician.')

The Financial

- how much money you want to earn and how you plan to earn it;
- how much money you want to save, how often you plan to save it (example: 'I save 20% of my gross income every week');
- the terms and conditions under which you will loan money to friends and family, if at all;
- how much money you want to spend and what you want to spend it on;
- how much money you want to give to charity and which charity you want to give it to;

- what investments you will and will not consider (example: 'I don't invest in pornography, companies with poor track record of sustainability, or any business that is illegal.')

What is involved in establishing a protocol?

- One way to establish a protocol is to have an experience yourself, feel the pain or the reward that comes from your choices, then vow to always do something or never do something in a particular way going forward.
- Another way to establish a protocol for yourself is to listen to, digest, and heed wise advice from someone else who knows more and/or has seen more than you. You borrow someone else's experience, knowledge, courage, or perspective from them and apply it into your situation.
- Remember that in order to benefit from the establishment and use of a protocol you need to make them in advance, before you get ambushed, unprepared to make an important choice, and before the resulting painful experience has you grumbling and swearing out of the side your mouth.

For example, if you want to be in good financial shape in the future, you might create a protocol for yourself that says: *I always earn more than I spend.* This protocol would benefit you in good times and bad, and help you avoid rough patches that you could create for yourself through credit card debt.

Furthermore, following this protocol could provide you a cushion to handle rough economic times that you had no hand in creating. You would have savings and investments to ride out the storm.

I'm going to offer some Old Money protocols for you to consider, but creating Advance Protocols is really going to be your personal work over your lifetime. Some of these will govern your life at a specific point in time—as a single woman, for example—and some of them will serve you well from now until, you know, age 85. These protocols are your guidelines. They will elevate and moderate your behavior through any and all circumstances. If you lose everything, they will help you maintain your dignity. If you have unbelievable success, they will help you accept your rewards and recognition with grace.

They will help you avoid mistakes and handle mistakes. They will help you create and hold a poised equilibrium which is the mark of a highly evolved, principled individual.

Old Money Protocols

Let's go through a few protocols that Old Money Gals frequently hold dear, generation after generation, with consistently rewarding results:

- *I always earn more than I spend.* Student debt is too often a fact of life and job prospects can be meager. Paying your bills can be a challenge, but you must draw the line at credit card debt. Hold fast to this protocol and you will prosper over the long haul. Every OMG I know is on a budget, regardless of how much money they have. They have a certain income, either from their work or their investments (or both) and they spend less than that every month. No exceptions.

- *When I leave the house, I'm dressed.* This protocol means that when you step out your front door, you're presentable. You're dressed to the point that you'd be comfortable if you accidentally met the person of your dreams or a business colleague who could facilitate you landing the position of your dreams. Don't get caught in sweatpants and flip-flops with bed-head. OMG's just don't step out sloppy. "You never know who you'll run into," is the common refrain. 'Presentable' is the standard.

- *I'm always reading a worthwhile book.* You've heard the saying that the difference between men and boys is the price of their toys. Well, the real substance of a woman is not so much in her looks, but in her books. Not reading is the same as not eating vegetables: you're not being nourished. As one OMG put it, "God help you if someone asks you what you're reading and there's silence. Disastrous. You've lost."

- *I do what needs to be done, when it needs to be done, whether I like it or not.* This is the central point of getting an education: being given a task and seeing it through, pleasant or not. This is the discipline and rigor that informs Old Money culture. Everyone is in the habit of taking care of business, with focus and passion, and then getting on to having a gin and tonic. (Just joking about that last part. Sort of.)

- *I am selective about who I share my bed with.* Rushing into sex exposes you to all sorts of unnecessary risks, pregnancy and sexually transmitted diseases being the most obvious. Less obvious is the damage such behavior does to your self-esteem, reputation, and relationships.

- *I don't loan money.* The old saying goes that loaning a friend money is a sure way to lose both. Know it. That is not to say you can't be generous. If a friend needs money, give it to them if you feel it's the right thing to do. Just don't expect to ever see the money again. If you can't afford to give it to them, you damn sure can't afford to loan it to them. Frequent Old Money response to a request for a loan: "I'm sorry. That's not something that I do."

- *If I'm going to make a purchase of $100.00 or more, I think it over.* This means no impulse shopping. If you're going shopping, know exactly what you're going to buy and why you're going to buy it. No shopping when you're upset. No shopping just because you're bored. This one comes from an OMG I know whose family net worth is in eight figures. She and her husband discuss any purchase they're considering that's over one hundred dollars. "Half the time, after talking about it, we decide not to buy it, whatever it is." Moral of the story: if she takes the time to think about it, you can take the time to think about it. A secondary measure is to pay actual, physical cash for things. If you see something in a store and want to buy it, pay cash. If you don't have the cash, take the trip to the bank or ATM and pull out the cash you need to buy the item. Then return to the store and hand over your hard-earned cash for a material possession. (Or just leave your credit cards at home.) If you follow this back-up protocol, you won't buy half of what you would spontaneously with a credit or debit card.

- *I exercise 5 times a week.* Let's be realistic: most people won't exercise everyday, even though they'd like to. So just make a commitment to exercise three weekdays out of five, and then on Saturday and Sunday, when you probably have more time. Old Money is healthy. It's not an accident.

- *I only do business with people I know, or through a referral from someone I know.* You can also expand this protocol to include people you date and socialize with, but note that the quality of your experience with this protocol will depend upon the quality of the people you know. So you may have to improve your circle of friends and colleagues to get the full benefit of this protocol. Nevertheless, it will limit your exposure to amateurs and hustlers.

- *I prioritize my savings...and my spending.* Today, many women prioritize savings. They set aside a percentage of their net income on a consistent basis in order to build a nest egg for savings and investment. That's great. You also want to prioritize your spending. Know this: what you spend your money on, above and beyond the necessities like food and shelter, defines you. Make your priorities education or self-improvement, then travel, then material possessions. Books can be a window to the world; travel is the world itself. While you are working and saving money, read. When you have some discretionary funds, travel. See how other people in other lands live, work, and love. When you spend your money on travel, you become richer for it.

~ OLD MONEY SECRET ~

The better your decision making process, the better the results of those decisions, and the higher your overall quality of life. Establishing protocols—set-in-stone rules, boundaries, procedures, or points of reference that inform and shape choices—contributes to consistently good decision-making.

* * * * * * * *

THINGS TO REMEMBER

When people older and more worldly than you offer advice, they are often trying to *lend you their experience* without you being *required to pay for it* with money, suffering, or lost opportunity. If the advice is sound, if it is relevant to your situation, if you accept it, and if you act on it properly, consider yourself fortunate to benefit from their wisdom without acquiring it through experience. This is a rare occurrence and a blessing.

The protocols you adopt and adhere to will form your own personal 'code' that you live by. They will act as a blueprint as you design and build your life, and they will be a personal support system when you face difficult situations.

When you find yourself in an unfamiliar situation, your decisions will be easier to make. If you established a set-in-stone protocol in advance, you don't have to 'decide'. The decision has already been made for you.

If someone makes a request that you're not comfortable with, it may not be pleasant to say: "*That's not something I do.*" It will, however, enable you to deliver the bad news as a matter of policy, not something personal.

On the other side of that coin, when someone learns that it's a protocol of yours to, let's say, double check all of your work, it will instill confidence. It will also tilt the scales in your favor should a controversy ever arise: your protocol has already been established and communicated to others. *Everybody knows how you roll.*

Protocols are not just walls to keep trouble at bay: they are bridges that connect you to those who share your values, and may even share some of your protocols. You won't need to broadcast or pontificate, just adhere to your protocols. Your actions will tell everyone everything they need to know.

Articulating, establishing, and implementing life-long protocols can be challenging and may be isolating at times. Do it anyway. Construct protocols wisely. Adopt them deliberately. Live by them always. Even if it's difficult. As we've noted, you must embrace pain and use it as fuel for your journey.

EXEMPLAR – PRINCESS DIANA

It is impossible to speak completely about the life of Princess Diana and its impact in these few paragraphs. However, let me give you a glimpse. Although famous for marrying into the Windsor family, she was a blue blood in her own right as a descendent of the Spencer family, who've been around for centuries.

She cut her own path, shocking the establishment and transforming public attitudes when, in 1987, she sat on the bed of a man with HIV/AIDS and held his hand. Most celebrated for her charity work and for her support of the International Campaign to Ban Landmines, Diana was also involved with dozens of charities, including London's Great Ormond Street Hospital for children.

She also raised awareness and advocated ways to help people affected with HIV/AIDS, cancer, and mental illness. Her influence and ability to direct attention—and support—to any charity she became involved with made her a powerful force for good. Charities that worked to combat cancer, drug abuse, and homelessness in the UK and abroad all benefited from her generosity and well-used celebrity.

If you have the opportunity to give of your time and your money, learn more about the life of Princess Diana.

> *"Carry out a random act of kindness, with no expectation of reward, safe in the knowledge that one day someone might do the same for you."*
>
> –PRINCESS DIANA

"Our greatest glory is not in never falling,
but in rising every time we fall."

—Confucius

August 13, 2016—Verona, Italy

CHAPTER 8

Through The Looking Glass

In this chapter, we're going to discuss ideals and illusions. An ideal is the perfect and complete embodiment of a concept, its supreme collection of attributes, qualities, or abilities. An ideal articulates a target, an aspiration. An illusion is the inaccurate interpretation of something or someone we see, think we know and understand, something we assign value to, something we experience, or something we erroneously accept as true.

In a form of government, many people hold up as an 'ideal' the concepts of equality, democracy, shared values, and the rule of law. For example, when the United States' Founding Fathers drafted the Declaration of Independence, they asserted that 'all men are created equal'. This was one of the 'ideals' they set forth. At the time these words were written, however, the inconvenient truth is that many of these men were slave owners. 'Equality' obviously did not apply to their slaves; it did not apply to women, to Native Americans, or even to other white men who did not own property.

Nevertheless, we still hold these words and this concept—that all men are created equal—as our ideal in the United States. It has pushed us forward and made us better. Women, Native Americans, and African Americans now have the right to vote, own property, and marry who they wish. Racial discrimination in the workplace and in education is illegal. The LBGT community makes progress toward more equal rights, based on this ideal.

Ideals fall short of 'reality', but they are held up by society as goals to which we should aspire. They elevate thought and action. We need them. They benefit us. We may, one day in a perfect world, achieve an ideal. More likely is that we will keep them in mind as we make imperfect progress.

On a personal level, you may have a role model or an 'ideal' of what you want to achieve in your career or who you want to become as a person. You may have an 'idol' who has your 'dream job' or lives your 'dream life'. While you know this person is human, that they have faults that you don't want to adopt and private challenges that you don't know about, you still hold them up as your role model of what you want to become. What you do with this ideal person is look at how they got to where they are, and see if you can follow a similar path. You model the positive behaviors you see them exhibit: hard work, dedication, skill, creativity, professionalism, grace, and generosity.

If you have a concept as an ideal, you may turn that into your mantra. For example, if you want to be a successful novelist, you might say something like, 'I'm going to be the next J.K. Rowling.' This doesn't mean you dye your hair blonde and speak with a Scottish accent. It means you strive to create a great work of fiction that readers the world over enjoy.

The thing you do with an ideal is internalize it, keep it to yourself, and let it silently govern your behavior.

Over time, it is a universal law that what you think about constantly and work toward persistently will become real, although sometimes not in the way you've imagined. In this truth lies the importance of having an ideal and pursuing it.

The Illusion

An illusion is an inaccurate opinion, belief, or impression, something that we believe to be true, but that is, by evidence and experience, not true. While an ideal is something we work toward, an illusion is something we cling to. It is a something that we often desperately want to be true, need to be true, or hope to be true, but don't make any effort to make true. For example, if you say you want to be the next J.K. Rowling, but you're not sitting down almost every day and writing, if you're not then taking what you've written and pursuing agents and publishers, then you may be suffering from an illusion about being a famous writer.

Note: it often feels better to us to have an illusion about something or someone than to acknowledge the reality and act to change it.

Another example of an illusion that is particularly prevalent among many women is the image they have of their body as it relates to the images that are presented to them in the media. Photographs of picture-perfect celebrities or fashion models whose hair, face, figure, and wardrobe are always perfect, create the illusion that this is 'real' and that it is attainable by all women everywhere. The truth about these images, and these celebrities or models, is less glamorous. They are acutely aware that they have chosen a very competitive profession. They commit themselves. They work with acting, singing and diction coaches. They regularly work with personal trainers. They hire chefs to make sure they eat well. They have assistants to handle their schedules and maximize their time.

They know that their image is a major part of their career. Regardless of how hard they work, they need to appear relaxed, elegant, and charming in public. To support this appearance, they have stylists for their hair, personal shoppers for their clothes, publicists for their interviews and appearances, and cosmetic surgeons to provide a little nip and tuck to keep them looking 'youthful'.

So it's unrealistic to think that they 'have it all together' all the time. After a lot of work by a lot of people, they 'have it together' on the red carpet or on screen for a limited period of time. Projecting an effortlessness to it all that belies all the hard work is part of their job: creating an illusion. What's more, when a photo of them does appear on the internet or in a magazine, it has been retouched by editorial professionals to minimize or eliminate any imperfections and provide a final touch or two of radiance and sparkle. No wonder these women look great. With a team of professionals at their beck and call, they should look great.

This aspect of the entertainment and fashion industries is what it is. These women are in the business of selling dreams: movies, television shows, clothes, and cosmetics. The problem begins when young women and working women are constantly exposed to these carefully manufactured creations. It's tempting to believe that these artificial creations are the norm, the standard, the rule.

Old Money Gals who embrace the Old Money, New Woman philosophy, who work for a living and use their resources wisely, don't compare their bodies or their look with the size zero, flawless prototypes that are constantly presented as the 'ideal'. Old Money Gals know instinctively that this illusion is not any kind of 'ideal'. They don't aspire to this. They don't imitate this. They aren't envious of this. They aren't influenced by this.

Some celebrities have sensed this disconnect and addressed it. In 2016, for example, the singer/songwriter Alicia Keys started the #nomakeup movement to address the struggles and pressures to 'look a certain way' that many women face. She vowed to stop covering up: 'Not my face, not my mind, not my soul, not my thoughts, not my dreams, not my struggles, not my growth. Nothing.' Assess her decision and see how or if it makes sense to you. Moderate your exposure to images of an 'ideal' that are predicated on appearance. Do not make yourself crazy in the pursuit of an illusion. While an illusion is a dangerous thing to have about a goal or a situation, it can be positively devastating to have it about a person. As I said, an ideal is something we keep to ourselves. Conversely, an illusion is something we project onto another situation or person. You may already know these things, but it's critically important now that you *understand them and apply them to your life, both at work, in relationships, and in love.*

Don't labor under the illusion that your life is just going to 'turn out fine' because you daydream about it but don't work at it; that you're 'entitled' to a pay increase at work just because you've been at your job for a couple of years; or that the slacker you're dating is going to magically evolve into an ambitious young man just because you continue to love and (financially?) support him.

The reason I say these harsh things is because I have seen too many women have illusions about the world, and about their partners, that permanently impact their lives in unpleasant ways. When these women see the reality about the situations and partners they have become involved with, or the financial choices they have made, they are often left with few viable options. They face divorce, debt, children to care for, and careers to jumpstart late in the game or rebuild with limited resources, and often have little time, money, or strength to change or improve their situations.

I don't advocate approaching life and love like a business, looking at the risk/reward ratio in every friendship or romance through a transactional lens. I also don't advocate approaching life and love as a fairy tale, thinking that a happy ending will surely turn up, somehow, someday. When you take the time to invest in yourself and learn who you are and what's important to you, you'll be more likely to determine what your 'ideal' or 'ideals' are in life. You'll also be less susceptible to illusions, whether they involve material possessions or other people.

The things you consider important will be more intangible, like purpose, work, and integrity, but more meaningful. Superficial things that are advertised and promoted will hold less appeal and carry less weight. When this shift in your thinking occurs, you will be able to face 'reality' with less trepidation and 'own' your future. Tell yourself the truth and live accordingly.

Now that we've addressed some illusions on the personal front, let's discuss some illusions that appear in relationships.

The 'Knight in Shining Armor' Syndrome

You may have an *ideal* partner that you want in your life in the future, probably as boyfriend, girlfriend, lover, partner, or husband. Good. That's your ideal. Hold that thought. What you may have articulated, in your mind and maybe in your diary, is a list of characteristics. Your ideal partner has these characteristics, and they're important to you. Some can be superficial, like hair color—or the requirement that they simply have hair—and some are incredibly important, like kindness and honesty.

As you go through life with this 'ideal love' list in your mind, you'll meet candidates who have a few, some, or many of the physical characteristics or personality traits that you want in a partner. It is probable that no one person will have all of them. Do not despair: you will discover that you can live quite happily without one or two things on your list. I will offer this advice: be careful what you wish for. Be more careful what you settle for.

Conversely, you may be dating or in love with someone right now and have *illusions* about who they really are or what they are really going to become. This is trouble. How do you know if you're harboring an illusion? Ask yourself some questions that relate to what you want, expect, and hope for from them:

- Are they reliable?
- Are they a 'finisher'?
- Are they saving money?
- Do they have a mentor?
- Do they value an education?

- Are they planning or starting a new venture?
- Are they socializing with ambitious and honorable people?
- Do they have a plan? For the near future? For the long term?
- If you think they're going to be successful, are they working hard right now?
- Do their daily actions match up with what you believe to be true about them?

If you believe they love you:

- Are they loyal?
- Are they considerate?
- Are they unkind to you?
- Do they communicate?
- Are they physically or verbally abusive to you?
- Do they know what's important to you?
- Do they support you in your endeavors?
- Do they treat people you care about with respect, even if they don't always agree with them or even like them?
- Are they harboring illusions of their own? Have you spoken with them about these? How did they respond?
- Is there evidence in their daily behavior and would there be testimony from your family and friends that would support your beliefs about them?

Most of these are 'yes or no' answers. If's, and's, or but's don't cut it. No rationale. No justifications. Does the person you love walk the walk? Do their actions match up with your ideals, for the most part? If not, you may be suffering from an illusion. You must decide.

Note: fall in love head first.

Ideals, Illusions, and Old Money

Old Money individuals and families often have ideals. Parents impart these ideals to their children and reinforce them through the following:

- *example*: a good example is worth a thousand lectures, as I always say. I also say that a good example is extremely irritating. But that's beside the point;
- *education*: to be well educated, in the formal sense and also the more practical sense, to learn not *what* to think but *how* to think;
- *exposure*: to a variety of people, foreign countries, and unique experiences, which is the opposite of living a sheltered life.

The parents act with integrity in their private and public lives. They are fair with family members and friends. They know and adhere to a simple truth: your ideals elevate your life while your illusions sabotage your life. They set an example that their children can see, even if their children ignore what their parents say.

As I said previously, Old Money families advocate an education, often rigorous and no-nonsense, so their children are prepared for the real world. There is an old saying that I heard as a child—numerous times—from my father: "I'd rather things be difficult for you growing up than difficult for you as an adult." Getting an education can be difficult, for the parent and for the child, but a well-rounded, educated individual is an ideal (one that is within reach, actually) that benefits the individual, the family, and society in equal measure. Old Money families also endorse exposure, often through travel and work, to challenge assumptions, to experience new environments, so that their children can learn, mature, develop new skills, see what life is really like, and discover who they really are. Mistakes and pain are part and parcel to this process. So are adventures, accomplishments, and a forged core of self-confidence and personal identity that the latest trends and the opinions of others will not quickly alter or weaken.

Note: when there is a certain emotion felt about something, and the evidence regarding that same thing is contradictory, Old Money discounts the emotion and heeds the evidence, painful as it may be.

What Old Money doesn't tolerate is illusion. Not about themselves and certainly not about other people. Everybody won't like you. So what? Everything won't be perfect all the time. Work, even when you love it, is sometimes challenging. People are sometimes contradictory and baffling. Life can seem unfair. And it often is.

Things that really matter and really have value can't be bought. What's more, they often take effort to acquire and maintain. To manifest an ideal, or anything close to it, requires focus and discipline. This pursuit is never without disappointment and defeat, but remember, 'the greatest glory is not in never falling, but rising every time we fall.'

~ OLD MONEY SECRET ~

> Old Money holds its ideals dear, but does not tolerate illusions. Old Money is keenly aware that there is a fine line between an ideal and an illusion. An ideal is a concept in its perfect and complete state, aspired to over time, a goal to work toward. An illusion is a misunderstanding of attributes or conditions, a danger to recognize, avoid, or discard as soon as possible.

* * * * * * * *

Things To Remember

People are on their own path. It is rare that you can alter the direction of that path, or the destiny that awaits a particular person, no matter how much you care for that person. If you try to change that person's path, you get off your own path and may lose your way. That doesn't help either of you.

If you can recognize that path by looking at past behavior, environmental factors, and aspirations that are honored by actions (usually hard work and persistence), you can decide how involved you want to be in someone's life, and determine how to be involved in their life, without illusions.

People aren't as original and unique as they think they are. They come from a certain culture and a certain social class that imprints behaviors and priorities on them, and these cultures and classes also have expectations of them. Few people escape these expectations. If you live long enough, pay attention just a little, and remain authentic to who you are, you can meet someone, and, in a relatively short period of time, have a good idea of who they are, where they're going, and what obstacles they're going to face along the way. Again, you can also decide if you want to be around for—or involved in—any of it.

It's not being cynical. It's certainly not being naive. It's being smart as you move toward being wise. Again: embrace your ideals. Harbor no illusions.

Exemplar – Leontyne Price

The year was 1927. Construction began on Mount Rushmore. Charles Lindbergh completed the first solo flight across the Atlantic. "The Great Mississippi Flood", the most destructive flood in US history, hit the southeastern part of the country. And on February 21, in the small town of Laurel, Mississippi, Leontyne Price was born.

The granddaughter of two Methodist ministers in the deeply segregated South, Ms. Price began singing in church. When she was five or six years old, her parents purchased her a toy piano. "I was center stage from the time I received that toy piano…I had the disease then," said Ms. Price later in life.

Ms. Price was an excellent student at Oak Park Vocational High School and later enrolled at the College of Education and Industrial Arts in Wilberforce, Ohio. She focused broadly on music education, but the faculty, aware of the gift she possessed, persuaded her to concentrate on voice. After graduation, she left for New York City to attend The Juilliard School on a full scholarship.

At Juilliard, Ms. Price studied under the tutelage of her beloved vocal instructor, Florence Page Kimball. Ms. Price's beautiful lyric soprano voice landed her feature roles in many of the school's operas. During this time, composer Virgil Thomson saw one of her performances and immediately cast her in one of his productions.

Ms. Price rose to international fame during a period of racial unrest in the 1950s and 60s. In 1955, when she was engaged to sing the lead for the NBC's production of Puccini's *Tosca,* some local affiliates were outraged and refused to air the performance. Nevertheless, her dramatic portrayal and unparalleled vocal performance were a critical success. Other televised operatic roles soon followed with her performance of Verdi's Aida for the first time in 1957. Her success led her to perform in Vienna, and in 1960, to the stage of La Scala, opera's most revered venue.

Ms. Price was the first American of African descent to become a leading prima donna at the Metropolitan Opera in New York City.

Her honors are numerous: the Presidential Medal of Freedom (1965), the Kennedy Center Honors (1980), the National Medal of Arts (1985), numerous honorary degrees, and nineteen Grammy Awards, including a special Lifetime Achievement Award in 1989, more than any other classical singer. She received one of the first Opera Honors given by the National Endowment for the Arts in 2008.

Ms. Price came from an Old Money family who valued education and the arts. She went on to become one of the most acclaimed musical artist of the 20th century, in spite of the prejudice and segregation that haunted America during the 1950s and 1960s.

Her voice is something words cannot describe, only ears can truly appreciate, and only hearts can understand. Suffice to say that at her final performance at the Metropolitan Opera House in New York City, her lifelong commitment to her art was truly appreciated. The audience gave her a standing ovation...which lasted for half an hour.

If you love music and think you might commit your life to it, listen to the work of Leontyne Price and be inspired. Read more about her and her career.

"Who I am is the best I can be."

–Leontyne Price

"Wait not for permission, advice, or affirmation from others to pursue what you want."

—Anonymous

June 9, 2017—O' Cebreiro, Spain

CHAPTER 9

Born Ready

This is the first of three chapters that we'll categorize as 'Presentation', the definition of which is simply the manner in which you present yourself to the world. Under the 'Presentation' umbrella, we'll first address 'Preparation'. We'll follow that with a chapter on 'Comportment' and then 'Clothing and Grooming'. We'll isolate and discuss these elements separately because there is much to be said about each. So, first things first.

Preparation, to be precise, is the extent to which you have made yourself ready to competently and confidently execute a certain task or ready yourself for a particular event. Whether it's for a piano recital or a basketball game, it is important that you prepare and that you prepare in the correct manner. If, prior to a recital, you spend two hours on your hair, makeup, and wardrobe, but don't spend time practicing the piano, you probably won't perform well. You won't 'present yourself' well overall. You may have presented yourself well with regard to your appearance, but you have not *prepared* to execute the task of playing the piano well. Let's look at preparation in other familiar situations:

In high school, preparation is a straightforward issue: you show up—mentally and physically—listen to teachers, learn lessons, take notes, and read textbooks in order to be prepared to take and pass exams. As you move onward and upward with your education, you (hopefully) engage with more sophisticated concepts in order to understand how they relate to your world.

In college, you show up, encounter more complex subjects like philosophy and applied mathematics. These enrich your life and may, again, *prepare* you for life after university, both as a professional with a career and a well-rounded human being with a core base of knowledge.

In the business world, there's the job interview. You show up—prepared. You've researched the company you want to work for. You've learned about their executives and their industry and perhaps talked with people who currently work there.

In your career, if you prepare extensively, you will be deemed credible, competent, informed, skilled, or even an expert. You will develop the skills to do what you say you can do, whether it's painting a fresco or forecasting next quarter's profit margins.

Those are some of the benefits of being prepared. You should also know there is a price for being unprepared. First, you probably won't be given a second chance to return to the recital or the business meeting and do it all over again. Life doesn't work like that: it's too competitive. People don't have the time. Furthermore, many times it will be men who sit in judgment of how well you have prepared. Despite their best attempts at being fair, they may still harbor a conscious or subconscious bias against women. You, as a woman, may be required to be 'extra-prepared' in order to compete against men who may be less prepared, less qualified, less talented. I'm not telling you anything new, especially if you're a woman of color.

It is, however, important to know this: your preparation or lack thereof reflects not just on you, but on *all women* who interview for a job, who make a presentation, who play at a recital. If you're not as prepared as you can be, you will confirm the prejudices of men who assess your work. You will disappoint the women who have come before you, who have been prepared and have excelled. You will also betray and disadvantage the women who come after you, who have prepared, but now face unfair judgments against them because you, as a woman, weren't prepared. Be prepared.

Social Norms

In closing this chapter, let me just touch on a few points that relate to preparation in your social life.

Know that punctuality is a key habit to develop, obviously when it comes to business meetings and appointments, but also with dates and dinner parties. Waiting on a woman who is not your wife has little charm. Be on time by planning to be on time. Get ready. Leave early. Arrive safely. Old saying: early is on time; on time is late; and late is unacceptable.

For social occasions, preparation also means you've gleaned some idea about the event and the guests, what you should wear, where the venue is located, how you're going to get there—transportation, traffic issues, and directions, and what you should bring as a gift for the hosts. (You should always bring a gift.)

Being prepared also applies to conversation. Let's say you're meeting a potential dating partner for the first time to have a cup of coffee. You might take a look at the morning's headlines first. This will give you something to talk about that's above gossip, but not quite as elevated as quantum physics. You might also be prepared to discuss the book you're reading. (You are reading a book right now, aren't you?) And you'll have some questions in mind that you'll want to ask about the other person. These fundamentals will help the conversation flow and allow everyone the chance to put their best foot forward.

Note: I would caution you about searching online to gather information in advance about someone you're going to meet on a social or romantic basis. "Oh, yes, I Google'd you," is hardly a sparkling opener. Call me old fashioned (again), but I think people might like to be taken at face value. Engage in the magic of meeting someone new without preconceived ideas gathered from internet search results.

Remember: preparation is the key that opens all doors.

Exemplar – Ada Byron King

Ada Byron King, Countess of Lovelace, the only legitimate child of the poet Lord Byron, seemed destined for fame at birth. Her determined mother spearheaded Ada's rigorous education, which focused on music, mathematics, and science.

In 1833, the young countess met an English math professor at Cambridge University named Charles Babbage. Despite their more than 25 year age difference, they were intellectual peers and became fast friends. Babbage, who would become known as 'the father of computers', corresponded with the countess for the next two decades, during which time he invented what was called the 'Analytical Engine'.

In 1843, Babbage asked her to translate a description of his engine for an Italian military engineer. Over the next nine months, she did just that...and more. In addition to providing a literal translation, she added her own set of notes which was three times longer than the actual translation. Her notes included some of Babbage's own calculations in which she found errors, made note of, and corrected.

She also possessed vision, describing how this 'Analytical Engine' could be used to calculate a sequence of figures, then proved the calculation by diagramming the computations that the machine would make. In short, she had written the first computer algorithm. She also saw the capability of computers to go beyond mere calculating, but also articulated how individuals and society might relate to technology as a collaborative tool.

The countess is considered by many to be the first author of a computer program, despite having lived a century before the invention of the modern computer. In 1953, more than a century after her death, her notes on Babbage's Analytical Engine were republished. The 'engine' has now been acknowledged as a prototype for a computer. Her notes are now regarded as the first description of a computer and software.

Ada Byron King, Countess of Lovelace, was a pioneer in computing. She championed the new technology that would shape the future.

If you want to join the increasing number of women innovators in STEM (science, technology, engineering, math) fields, consider the work of Ada Byron King.

"My comprehension can only be an infinitesimal fraction of all I want to understand."

—Ada Byron King

"If you're trying to be normal,
you'll never know how amazing you can be."

—MAYA ANGELO

July 14, 2017, the Marais, Paris

CHAPTER 10

Walk This Way

We've just discussed Preparation. Our next topic under 'Presentation' is 'Comportment', the manner in which you comport yourself: the way you walk, speak, and interact with others, both verbally and nonverbally. This includes posture, your diction and voice, etiquette and manners, and the mannerisms you use when you're talking or listening to someone. Comportment speaks volumes, before you ever utter a word.

It's important to understand that we're starting from 'the inside' and moving 'outward.' We began with Preparation, the work you do before you step outside your front door or present yourself or your skills to the outside world. This is the 'work', the process no one else really sees.

In this chapter on Comportment, we'll discuss how you carry yourself, after you're prepared. The way that you carry yourself and generally conduct yourself will remain constant, regardless to whether you've just put on a ball gown for an evening out or just finished a ball game with friends.

As I've mentioned, the third important aspect of Presentation is 'Clothing and Grooming': these things will be discussed last because these are things you can easily change. Being prepared and carrying yourself with grace and a certain reserve are things that you must work at. Know this: it is you who must decide, based on your goals and objectives in life, what 'being prepared' means for you. You must decide what image of yourself you're most comfortable with, and how much preparation is associated with that. That preparation will extend to how you carry yourself...and how you present yourself to the world. I'm simply highlighting some strategies to get you started. So...do the work first. Worry about appearances later.

A key part of Comportment is posture, the position in which you hold your body upright, against gravity, while walking, standing, or sitting. Posture communicates confidence and dignity, or the lack thereof. It is also important for your health, as it impacts the function of nerves and the flow of blood through the body. An easy mental exercise to help with posture is to imagine that a string runs through your spine and that an invisible hand is gently pulling the string through the top of your head, straightening your spine effortlessly, lifting your chin up. Once you visualize that, let your body react to the image, and hold that posture. That's your default position, sitting, standing or walking. Yoga will strengthen your torso and make good posture easier. You may want to find a yoga regimen that works for you and practice it daily, first thing in the morning. Personally, I do the Five Tibetans each morning. 15 minutes, 5 poses, good to go. You can find photos and instructions online if you're interested.

Now, let's talk generally and briefly about your health. You can't carry yourself with dignity and confidence if you're lethargic from sitting at your desk or on the sofa all day. You need to adopt an exercise program that works for you. Recently, a doctor was asked what the best kind of exercise was for a person to do. His answer was brilliant: the best kind of exercise for a person to do is the exercise they will do every day.

Let me give you some options that, combined with yoga, will help you feel better, live longer, and accomplish more. Fortunately, they don't require a personal trainer, gym membership, or Olympic-level skill set.

Weights. Using light weights consistently (1 to 3 pounds each) will give your arms some shape and tone, which is nice if you like to wear sleeveless dresses or punch your brother on a regular basis. Look online for an easy routine that keeps your shoulders, biceps, and triceps in good shape. Light weights, lots of repetitions equals tone without bulk. Heavy weights with fewer reps will pump you up. Use weights with those realities in mind.

Walking. A brisk walk several miles a day is great exercise which doesn't cost a dime. It will strengthen your legs and torso, as well as benefit your heart and internal organs. It also offers the opportunity to 'clear your head', provided you do it without earphones in your ears. Music may motivate you, but it prevents you from being completely aware of your surroundings when you're out in public, which is not always safe. A good walk, alone with your thoughts and unplugged from emails, phone calls, and social media is a good thing. Early morning is best. Think about it.

Bike. It's possible to pick up a stationary bike—used, often on Craigslist or yard sale—which can provide you with a great cardiovascular workout in 15 to 30 minutes of daily riding. If you live in a climate where bad weather can make outdoor exercise challenging to do every day, think about this option. Ride it every day, burn calories and sweat out whatever's bugging you. Watch self-improvement videos online as you ride in order to avoid getting bored and feeling like you're going nowhere. You are. (Wink, nod.)

In order to develop and maintain proper comportment, discipline will be required. You will need to be vigilant and aware about how you stand, walk, and sit. You will need to be consistent with exercise. However, the rewards in terms of health and appearance will last a lifetime.

Note: consult your doctor before beginning any physical regimen, then get your butt in gear.

To Be or Not To Be

Next, let's address behavior and mannerisms: if you've adopted a dumb-blonde, sex-kitten, militant-feminist, faux-intellectual, or any other personae, it's time to drop it. Shakespeare famously wrote that all the world's a stage and each of us play a part. It's fine to play your part, just be yourself as you do. It will be easier to remember your lines, take direction, and act with integrity.

Understand that people, not just women, sometimes behave in quite inauthentic ways in order to try to get attention, to be considered attractive, to be accepted, to protect themselves after getting hurt, or because they don't think their genuine personalities are good enough. Intelligent and aware adults see through these shallow performances and find them fatiguing, even if they're somewhat sympathetic to the emotional pain beneath them. So let's shelve the facades. Be confident enough in your genuine, getting-better-everyday-self to be who you are without pretense or affectation.

Recently, women have been encouraged to reject or mask their femininity in the workplace and adopt the worst behaviors of men: being rude, crude, pushy, or domineering. Resist this temptation. Be yourself. Be your best self. Use your femininity to your advantage. Strength, dignity, and grace are preferable. Avoid vulgarity. Don't be obnoxious or abusive.

Women don't have to 'grow a pair' in order to compete with men in business. Your awareness of who you are and the value you have—intrinsically as a person and with the skills you've developed as a professional—are your greatest assets. As a woman, you can open more doors with a smile than a threat.

Bring your 'lived experience' as a nurturer and giver of life to work. You don't have to be emotional, but you can certainly be empathetic. You can be effective without being artificial. Bring your insight and intuition into the boardroom. These 'feminine' attributes have tremendous value in business, politics, and society. Bring your insights. Bring your instincts. Know your stuff. Stand your ground.

Again, you can be competent and even tough in business (and life) without being vindictive, ruthless, mean, sarcastic, or nasty. Conversely, you don't have to act unintelligent. You can be attractive and even sexy without being overtly forward or flirty. The legendary jazz musician Miles Davis once remarked, "American women act like television." He was probably referring to overly dramatic and artificial behavior, something like you'd see on a soap opera. This is real life, not television. Don't act like television.

You can be courteous and kind and still send nonverbal signals through your posture, body language, and speech which give others, especially men, a very distinct idea of what behavior you will and won't tolerate. So, to paraphrase Shakespeare, it's your choice to discover your best self, to be that best self, and to that best self be true.

'Speak the language of the person you seek to become.'

—Anonymous

Self Defense

Sadly, I'm required to remind you that not all men acknowledge nonverbal signals, nor do they all respect women as they should. Violence against women is a global problem that you, as a woman, must be personally aware of.

Domestic violence, as the term implies, often refers to physical and emotional abuse that happens at home among family members. A common scenario is that the husband is violent with his wife. Should you find yourself in this situation, or even think you may be going in that direction, there are resources available to you, online, on the phone, down the street.

I am not going to discuss domestic violence in this book. I'm not qualified, and many other authors and professionals are. If you need help, use your power: click on the internet for expert assistance, call a trusted friend, or call 911.

The issue I will discuss briefly is personal safety and self-defense in public areas, where assault is usually unpredictable. The obvious truth is that men are many times physically larger and stronger than women. A man can restrain, attack, and harm a woman, simply because of this physical advantage. Again, sadly, this happens all too frequently.

As a woman, you must ask yourself the question, 'Would I be able to fight back if I were attacked?'. As a modern woman, you are working, socializing, and traveling, many times late at night and/or alone. You may have experienced a nervous, sinking feeling when walking alone at night, in a seemingly empty or poorly lit parking lot, or in an underground parking garage. Other situations include entering an apartment building, or, as a real estate professional, hosting an 'Open House' at a property where you are the only one on site until potential buyers arrive.

You may have been at social events with others in attendance when a man makes an unwelcome advance. You reject him, and he reacts in a threatening or violent manner. You may have extricated yourself from the situation, but, when you leave, you have the uneasy feeling that someone from the party might be following you—to your car or your place of residence.

In this situation, you may become upset and afraid. That's understandable. What you can't do is blame yourself for another person's behavior should they react poorly to your requirement for respect. What you can do is take precautions and be prepared.

Know this: if a man enters your personal space without your permission, you have the right to clear that personal space promptly, without apology or delay. Furthermore, a little *preparation and practice* can give you a sense of what you *could do* in the event that you were attacked. This will give you a measure of *confidence and competence*, which increases the likelihood that you'll respond effectively in the event someone assaults you.

More than expert technique, the willingness to fight is the priority with this issue. We've discussed not being a victim with regards to your finances and your health. This is not being a victim with regards to your personal safety. If you're a student, there are probably classes and information that can bring you up to speed with the basics of personal safety and self-defense. Seek them out. Pay attention. Take notes.

Find a self-defense technique or strategy that works for you. Get instruction from a professional. Practice. Get comfortable with the idea of protecting yourself. Learn to listen to your instincts and follow them.

Remember: you're learning to defend yourself from an attacker for a short, intense period of time. It's not a 15-round boxing match. It's a 30-second fight. You don't have to learn a lot. You just have to learn how to hurt someone enough so you can break free of him and run to safety.

The first lines of defense are: having girlfriends you trust with you when you're out; knowing the venue of the event you're attending and how to get to and from it safely; and finally, knowing who else is going to be attending an event. If you've got these three issues addressed, and you're comfortable with them, you're off to a good start.

Some other common-sense rules are as follows:

1. Avoid putting yourself in dangerous situations at all times;

2. Make sure you always have your cell phone with you AND that it's fully charged;

3. Have a friend, coworker, or relative take you to and wait for you if you have an evening or after hours appointment/interview at an unknown location;

4. Do not walk, jog or hike alone at night, or in an isolated area at any time;

5. Never, ever, ever go to a bar or attend a social event and leave alone after having drinks. Have an employee of the establishment or uniformed security guard walk you to your car. Wait inside near the exit for your taxi or Uber to arrive;

6. Keep gas in your car; do not run out of gas in a strange location;

7. If you are driving and your car fails, pull off the road, lock the doors, turn your emergency lights on. Call 911, a friend, or family member and wait for help to arrive. Only exit your vehicle when you see someone you've called that you recognize, or when you see a uniformed law enforcement officer in a marked vehicle;

8. If you're assaulted, be aggressive and loud. Kicking, hitting, and screaming may be all the self-defense technique you need in a situation.

Take time to discuss self-defense with your girlfriends and colleagues. Add to the list above and personalize it. Learn which local establishments (bars and clubs) are bad news for single women. Get the scoop from friends on mutual acquaintances (men) who have a reputation for ungentlemanly behavior. Avoid all of them.

As a final note, just remember to learn a few basic 'go-to' moves that will discourage an attacker. No matter the size of a man, his eyes, throat, and groin remain delicate and vulnerable. One strike to one of those areas can bring him to his knees, and the altercation to an end. Favor techniques that mesh organically with your instinctive responses. These defensive moves will come to you more quickly, and be executed by you more effectively, if you feel they're 'natural'.

It is my hope that you learn to defend yourself, and that you never have to defend yourself.

Etiquette and Manners

Let me first explain the difference between 'etiquette' and 'manners'. Etiquette is the set of written rules that govern civilized behavior, usually at the dinner table and at social functions. Etiquette concerns itself with the 'rules' that, for example, govern which forks to use while eating a five-course meal, or where to place your napkin when you're just getting up to go to the restroom, or leaving the table for the evening. Etiquette is the technical side of proper social behavior.

Manners are the more universal and more human aspect of good behavior. You can get a thing or two wrong about 'etiquette', but, if you're sincere and polite, you may be forgiven. Conversely, you can know every detail about how to hold your knife and fork and what to wear to an event when the invitation you've received is engraved, not just printed. But if you aren't kind, courteous, empathetic, and generous, you fall short of having 'manners'.

With that distinction out of the way, let me say that most everyone needs to improve their etiquette and manners. Buy a book on etiquette (Emily Post) and read it, then put what you've learned into practice.

Place a napkin in your lap at the dining table. Keep your elbows off that same dining table. Chew food with your mouth closed. Don't talk with food in that same mouth. Unless you're at an Indian restaurant and feeling native, use utensils to eat. Wait for everyone to be served before you start eating. At more formal affairs, wait for the host or hostess to start eating, or until they invite all the guests to begin, before you start eating. Be aware of the volume at which you speak and laugh.

On this last issue, I must interject a personal note. I live and work in Europe. As an American, it is discouraging how often I find myself glaring across an otherwise quiet restaurant at a group of *loud Americans*. It is irritating for Europeans, too, who generally sit, eat, and talk quietly, expecting to enjoy their meal in peace. As you embrace the Old Money, New Woman philosophy, please, please remember to be aware of the volume at which you speak and laugh, especially in public and especially when you travel abroad.

Don't use profanity. Don't chew gum. Speak articulately. Look online for videos or books that can help you improve your pronunciation and vocabulary. Elevate your standards. Repeat: elevate your standards.

When you meet someone for the first time, smile evenly and sincerely, introduce yourself, and shake hands. Make sure you've heard their name and confirm if there's confusion about this. Maintain a comfortable distance from them (approximately three feet). Engage in polite conversation. Ask questions. Listen. Be sincere. Don't have too much to drink. You'll be fine.

Also it's important to remember that a cornerstone of good manners is the use of thank you notes. Sadly, in an age of text and emails, this practice has fallen out of favor with many women. Revive it and hold it dear. Writing (with pen and ink) and mailing (through the post) a thank you note is an expression of gratitude, the dominant emotion of the universe. More practically, it is a polite way to express your appreciation to someone who has given you a gift, invited you to dinner, or provided you with a referral.

Yes, it takes time to sit down, write, stamp, and then mail a note to someone. That's the whole point: when someone receives the note, they'll appreciate that you took the time to write and send it. The quality of the paper and envelope is secondary. The maintenance of this tradition—the formal expression of gratitude—is essential for you, and for society. Champion it.

Ever The Diplomat

Someone once said that diplomacy is the art of telling someone to go to hell in such away that they look forward to the journey. As a woman, you should try your best in social situations to maintain your dignified comportment and be a diplomat. This diplomacy is simply a matter of you establishing the 'rules of the road' regarding behavior with every person you meet. You should be fair. You should also be unambiguous. Just as every diplomat is constantly aware of 'boundaries', so should the people who interact with you.

There are some boundaries to establish in various categories of your life. Considering them in advance will help you to be polite and more of a diplomat in responding when or if delicate situations ever present themselves. Here are a few:

In Business: are you going to get romantically involved with colleagues at work? Specifically, are you going to get involved with your boss or a person in a more senior position? Are you going to do something illegal or unethical in order to give you or your company an advantage? Have you considered all of the consequences of your actions?

In Love: are you going to sleep with someone on the first date? What requirements are you going make of someone who wants to date you? Are you going to be unfaithful to your partner? Are you going to allow them to be unfaithful or be abusive to you? Are you fine with the risks?

In Society: are you going to set standards about how you behave? Are you going to refuse to be seen at certain establishments (let's say, I don't know...dive bars, for example) or refuse to be seen with certain groups of people (let's say, I don't know...neo-Nazis, as an example)?

Situations may vary. Having well-established rules of behavior will enable you to do your best to be polite, be a diplomat, and not be caught off-guard. You might come up with some stock answers, in advance, to questions like, 'Hey, would you like to have a drink after work?' or 'We're meeting some friends at the Randy Dandy tomorrow night at midnight for shots and lap-dances. Wanna come?'

We'll discuss the decision-making process in a later chapter, but, thinking diplomatically, you might have your stock answers—'You know, that's just not something that I do, but thanks for asking'—in the back of your mind, and on the tip of your tongue. Again: most of this is simply about you establishing the 'rules of the road' about how you are treated and what you do and don't do, with every person you meet, at the start, with fairness, but without any ambiguity. So be friendly, be personable, be kind, but start your relationships with a certain formality and reserve. Require others to earn your trust, step by step. Be yourself, but be your best self. Some people will like you. Some won't. Accept this and move on.

Remember: if you're worried about being normal, you'll never know how amazing you can be. So don't be normal, but do be diplomatic.

Remember also: it is difficult for men to be gentlemen if women are not ladies. So, ladies, mind your manners and require manners, respect, and the best behavior from men. We will rise to the occasion.

To summarize, comportment is important. Carry yourself with grace and dignity at all times. This is a combination of being physically healthy, having good posture, and being centered as a person. Being 'centered' is the balance of being polite and being firm. Let your demeanor and vocabulary reflect this balance.

Exemplar – Corazon Aquino

Initially, Corazon Aquino was a homemaker, more interested in caring for her family and supporting her husband, Senator Benigno S. Aquino Junior, in his political career. However, when he was assassinated at the Manila Airport upon his return from exile, she could no longer remain silent, or on the sidelines.

In a snap election called by then president Ferdinand Marcos in 1986, Corazon Aquino became the first woman president of the Philippines. Marcos initially declared himself victorious until peaceful demonstrations across the country publicized and denounced the fraudulent election results. Corazon was finally acknowledged as the legitimate winner and took office in 1986.

She took the oath of office as the eleventh President of Philippines on February 25, 1986. Determined to root out corruption, she set up the Presidential Commission on Good Government, whose main task was to investigate and recover the ill-gotten wealth accumulated by previous regime.

She also abolished the existing constitution and appointed a commission to write a new one, which was ratified in 1987. In an act of true statesmanship, Aquino thought of her people first: she made sure that the new constitution severely limited—not the power of those who could challenge her rule—but the powers of her own office, the presidency.

This is courage. This is public service.

> *"I've reached a point in life, where it's no longer necessary to try to impress. If they like me the way I am, that's good. If they don't, that's too bad."*
>
> —Corazon Aquino

"Excellence is to do a common thing in an uncommon way."

—Booker T. Washington

February 21, 2017—Porto, Portugal

CHAPTER 11

Wear It Well

We've discussed Preparation. We've discussed Comportment. The final aspect of Presentation is your appearance: 'Clothing and Grooming'. The combination of these three aspects of Presentation is key as you prepare for this journey. This part of the package is no less important; it is simply the most visible.

Clothing and grooming are the first things a person notices when they meet you. Psychologists tell us that a person will make about a dozen visual observations and judgments in the first few seconds of meeting another person. That means, when someone is introduced to you for the first time, before you ever say a word, they've taken in and interpreted more than ten visual signals about you based on your appearance. They've looked at how you've dressed, if you've made any effort to dress, how tastefully you've executed that effort, and how appropriately dressed you are for the occasion. They will also consider how well or how poorly you've done your hair and makeup, the neatness and quality of your clothes, and your posture and composure.

These observations are then interpreted, given meaning and value, and then, like it or not, conclusions are drawn about you. It is probably unfair, but it is certainly true: people do judge a book by its cover, and a person by their appearance. The people you meet will equate the effort you've put into your appearance as being roughly equivalent to:

- the amount of respect you have for yourself;
- the respect you have for them and the value you've assigned to meeting them; and/or
- the importance you assign the event at which this meeting takes place.

To make the most of these moments, it is important to objectively assess how you look, not just to yourself in the mirror, but to others in public. Your journey to discover the best way to present yourself will be to find the 'look' that is 'you', whatever the occasion.

You'll identify and refine this 'look' more quickly, easily, and less expensively if you know your body and know what looks good on you, without regard to passing trends or fads. Look at photos from your past. Critique your look from a year ago, five years ago, ten years ago. Again, find the look that works for you and refine it.

There are some inevitable basics to this process. They include quality, well-maintained clothes and shoes, a good haircut without a wild style-and-dye job, and a classic manicure—fingernails neither neglected nor overdone.

A key Old Money, New Woman fundamental of 'dressing well' is 'dressing appropriately'. This is simply to know that what you wear is usually contingent upon the event you'll be attending or the activity you'll be participating in.

Before we go into detail, a final point: when you dress, it is important to consider your wardrobe as an 'ensemble'. 'Ensemble' is the French word for 'together', by the way. So if you want to look like you have it 'together', view the articles of clothing you wear as team members. An Old Money Gal knows that this team, coordinated from head to toe, will work together to project a single image, one that makes a good *presentation* and one that is *appropriate* for the occasion.

RIGHT PLACE, RIGHT TIME

With these ideas in mind, let's consider some familiar scenarios, or occasions, with some go-to ensembles that are appropriate for each.

The Professional Job Interview...in which the goal is to get hired and progress in your career. If you show up for a job interview at a major corporation in jeans and a too-tight sweater, it probably doesn't matter what credentials you have. The human resources executive is going to feel like you don't place any value on the meeting, or that you don't have a clue. Either way, they won't take the time to consider you seriously. They won't consider you at all.

Remember that, although corporate dress codes have been relaxed on 'casual Friday's' at some companies, dress codes for interviews remain formal. Professional standards still apply. In the same way, appropriate interview attire for a company may differ from the day-to-day attire worn by employees in the office of that company. Just because employees dress in 'business casual' attire when they arrive at work doesn't mean you show up in 'business casual' for a job interview.

This scenario is the domain of the navy, black, or dark grey business suit with a skirt. Some women will wear suits with pants. Know your industry and the company you're interviewing with before ditching the skirt and wearing the pants. A white blouse and black or navy closed-toe heels or pumps complete the look.

A Casual Social Event...in which the goal is to catch up with friends and meet new people—building relationships and having fun. If you show up at an afternoon neighborhood pool party in a short black dress, blown-out hair, industrial-strength mascara, and stilettos, you may garner some initial attention from the male attendees, but probably not the kind you want. You haven't dressed appropriately for the occasion. Other guests will probably think you're one brick shy of a load, or that you've taken on a new profession, at least part-time. As with all Clothing and Grooming choices, know the event, know the host, know the crowd.

The Casual Lunch Out...is the time and place for a cotton or linen blouse, a men's tuxedo shirt, cotton or linen pants or khakis, and casual shoes. Bring a sweater or shawl in case the restaurant is really proud of their air conditioning. Casual shoes are not athletic shoes. Flats or elegant, simple pumps are better than sandals and much preferred to ghastly flip-flops or clunky Birkenstock's. (Please, say 'No' to Uggs.) Jeans are acceptable if they are not torn and don't reveal too much. Wear a heel to dress them up. Showing skin between your blouse and your pants should be reserved for the lake, the beach, or poolside at a resort.

The Backyard Barbecue...at a residence in the daylight hours, is perfect for a simple cotton or linen summer top, with cotton or linen pants (long or short), jeans, and some casual sandals or flats. Again no sneakers, flip-flops, or Birkenstocks, and again a sweater, if you need it when the sun goes down.

The Important Introduction...is slightly more formal. A daytime example...Let's say you arrive to meet your boyfriend's parents for the first time. You've dressed in a clean, modest, and fairly traditional dress, or blouse and skirt, with sweater and pumps. That's a good start. It's an appropriate ensemble for the venue, whether it be a residence, restaurant, or country club. You've dressed to be considerate of your boyfriend, who's nervous as a long-tailed cat in a room full of rocking chairs. You're also conveying respect to his parents, who may become members of your family in the future. And you've dressed to communicate that you respect yourself. You feel good about yourself. The potential in-laws are impressed. And your boyfriend is appreciative. Easy rule: say to yourself 'If the situation were reversed, how would I like someone to dress or behave for me?'

The Evening Out...might be dinner at a restaurant, cocktails on the town, or an elegant dinner party at a residence. This calls for the Simple Black Dress. Simple does not mean dowdy or boring. The dress should flatter you. If well-made and well-tailored, it will serve you well for years and never go out of style. Not too low cut in front, and not too short in length, please. Accessories may include a cozy shawl, colorful scarf, classic clutch, grandmother's pearls, or a single great piece of jewelry.

Why is it important to dress well? Because you want your appearance to make a positive contribution to your image, not be a negative or a distraction. You want to give people a fair chance to get to know you for who you are (social situations), or what you can contribute (work situations), from a neutral or preferably positive starting point. Dressing tastefully is also a reflection of what is going on inside you. It communicates what you think of yourself.

Your appearance should visually communicate that you respect yourself, and that you require other people to respect you, first and foremost, before they make any other judgments about you. This is especially true with a first impression. You have to make dressing well (not necessarily dressing up) a habit.

Caveat: if you are a musician, artist, or writer, or working in the fashion industry, I am completely wasting my breath/ink/paper here. You will dress to express yourself (artist), or barely dress because you genuinely couldn't care less (writer or musician), or dress to impress (fashion). When you enter the entertainment aspect of any of these careers, you will sometimes dress in order to communicate an image and promote your brand. This is called 'wardrobe'. It's clothing for a performance. Remember that you need to live a real life, too, and dress for that as well.

Bottom Line: if you want to show respect to the people you care about or an important event, know what the occasion is and dress appropriately.

"Dress shabbily and they remember the dress,
dress impeccably and they remember the woman."

—Coco Chanel

Things To Remember

If you feel you need guidance to develop a style or a look, I suggest you start with research, then take time to think and consider, then move slowly into purchases. Avoid advertising, fashion blogs, and fashion magazines. Avoid 'best-dressed' lists, as they're usually composed of celebrities who have stylists to dress them and publicists to promote them. As discussed, very few buy their own clothes or have a real style of their own.

Instead, research online photos of Jacqueline Kennedy Onassis, Michelle Obama, Christiane Amanpour, Amal Clooney, Katherine Hepburn, Audrey Hepburn, Sophia Loren, and Princess Diana. These women are often referred to as 'style icons' because most of the time they have dressed in a classic, refined manner that transcends the eras in which they lived. Each of them expresses their own individual style, regardless of the occasion. As you look at their photos, you'll quickly be able to discern which ensembles they wore that remain timeless. You want to focus on the timeless outfits and implement that style, if not the actual garments, into your wardrobe. Since women come in different sizes and shapes, I encourage you to look for the icon with your body type and analyze how they made the most of their looks.

For the Old Money Gal, the watchwords of style are *simplicity* and *elegance*, in that order. Less really is more. You wear the clothes. They should not wear you. Function and comfort are part and parcel to your wardrobe today. Clothes must fit and wear well. They must last for years, not just for this fashion season. They must be appropriate for the life you are living on a daily basis. They must not be likely to go out of style.

Oscar Wilde once said that fashion is something so bad it has to be changed every six months. Listen to Mr. Wilde. Avoid fashion like the plague. Do research and develop your style. Keep it simple. Keep it traditional. Keep it elegant. When in doubt, lean toward the conservative. Less is more. Less is more. Less is more.

Note: Old Money Gals regard their clothes as investments. With that in mind, you might consider a 5% monthly 'set aside' from your net pay to invest in your wardrobe as good values on classic pieces become available. This is not for impulse shopping: this is for deliberate, strategic investing in pieces that will last decades: a slow approach to building a classic wardrobe. Watch for end-of-season sales. Don't feel compelled to purchase something every month. Keep your wardrobe 'set aside' money separate from your regular savings and investment funds. Be patient. Invest wisely. Look fabulous.

Exemplar – Coco Chanel

Coco Chanel is the founder and namesake of the iconic Chanel fashion brand. She's also acknowledged to be the first 'influencer' in women's fashion, as well as the first person to take a 'selfie'.

Glamorous as her later life appeared to the public, it didn't start out that way. After her mother's death, young Gabrielle was sent to an orphanage. Life for children there was harsh and accommodations spartan. It was, however, where she would learn to sew, a skill that would change her life, as well as the world of fashion.

Success came early after she constructed a dress from an oversized jersey sweater. When asked about where she got the dress by several people, being a savvy business woman, she capitalized on the opportunity and offered to make dresses for them. The cut was stylish, the color choice was bold for that time, associated only with periods of mourning. But Mademoiselle Chanel had a vision, and the 'little black dress' was born.

Declaring that, "Luxury must be comfortable, otherwise it is not luxury," she liberated women from the constraints of the "corseted silhouette" and introduced a sporty, casual chic as the feminine standard of style immediately after World War I. This clean, classic, and comfortable style of dress that has endured for almost a century made her famous around the world, and very rich. Still, she wasn't satisfied.

In the 1920s, Coco Chanel, as she was then known, launched her first perfume, Chanel No. 5, the first to feature a designer's name. Perfume "is the unseen, unforgettable, ultimate accessory of fashion. . . . that heralds your arrival and prolongs your departure," she once explained.

A prolific fashion creator, Mademoiselle Chanel extended her influence beyond couture clothing, expanding her design aesthetic to include jewelry and accessories, many marked with her famed interlocked-CC monogram.

The Depression of the 1930s and the outbreak of World War II forced her to close her once-thriving business. Rumors of her romantic involvement with a Nazi military officer during the occupation badly damaged her reputation. While never formally charged with collaborating, the charges nevertheless resonated with French citizens. She was convicted in the court of public opinion and went into self-imposed exile in Switzerland. But she was not finished.

At age 73 she made a triumphant return to the world of fashion with a line of timeless designs that wowed the public, even if they were initially panned by the critics. She worked relentlessly until her death in Paris at age 87.

If you love fashion and think you might want a career in the field, or if you want to 'start over' at any age, read more about the life of Coco Chanel.

"I don't do fashion. I am fashion."

—Coco Chanel

"You cannot discover new oceans unless you have the courage to lose sight of the shore."

—Andre Gide

November 21, 2016—Verona, Italy

CHAPTER 12

Best in Class

I call it Old Money Style. It's often called 'preppy', sometimes 'Ivy Style', referring to the Ivy League schools in the northeast region of the United States, where this mode of dressing originated almost a century ago. Whatever you call it, it's the way Old Money Gals have been dressing for decades.

This traditional, comfortable, discreet, and elegant manner of dress has endured, oblivious to the winds of fashion. It remains a benchmark. Use it as your North Star, should you find yourself at a loss for wardrobe direction. It exclusively involves natural fabrics, leans toward solid colors, and will serve you extremely well over the course of your life.

Should you adopt this style, people may not notice what you're wearing on a specific day, but they will over time come to consider you as always 'well dressed', regardless of whether they see you in the office, around the neighborhood, or at a social event.

Again: the way you dress is nonverbal communication. When you opt to dress as an Old Money Gal, your style is communicating some important ideas to others about you: you're confident about your future, secure enough not to have to attract attention strictly with your clothes, independent in your thinking, and unapologetic about your values. You convey the idea that your attributes go much deeper than what meets the eye, and that, in order to find out what those are, someone will have to take an interest and make an effort to get to know you. You're not on display for anyone's amusement, entertainment, or approval.

Furthermore, you establish yourself as a person uninfluenced by passing trends, someone who doesn't need the latest fashion to prop up her self-esteem. You're presenting yourself as someone with self-respect and traditional values—the opposite of arm candy. All these things are going to work in your favor as you make a first impression, and as you create an appearance that conveys how you expect to be treated: fairly and with respect.

Random thing to consider: you've seen family photos that are ten, twenty, or thirty years old. Fashions captured in these images can be ghastly and comical. That's because they are fashions. They are not style. You know who doesn't look silly? Old Money Gals. Because they dress in the same style for decades, from generation to generation, from cradle to grave.

~ OLD MONEY SECRET ~

How a woman presents herself to the world will determine to a large extent how she is treated by the world and what results she gets from the world. Presentation includes preparation, comportment and manners, and clothing and grooming.

* * * * * * * *

The Short List

If you are a college student, or just starting out in your career, you want to keep your style simple, economical, and classic. Here's a Short List of the basics you can acquire in order to present yourself stylishly for decades:

1. White or sky blue long sleeve,100% cotton and linen blouses;
2. Solid color 100% cotton short sleeve pullovers;
3. Solid color pullover or cardigan sweaters,100% wool or 100% cotton;
4. 100% linen or cotton long pants and shorts in solid colors;
5. Grey, black, or navy 100% linen or wool/cashmere blend pants;
6. Grey, black, or navy 100% linen or 100% wool skirts;
7. A classic black dress, mid-length;
8. Black high heel shoes with a closed toe, for office or dress;
9. Navy or tan pumps with a chunk heel, for walking comfortably;
10. Topsiders, sandals, or loafers, for casual;
11. Wool socks and cotton socks and hose, neutral, blue or black;
12. Blue or black blazer;
13. Blue, black, or grey business suit of good quality;
14. Navy, grey, or camel tan full-length 100% wool coat for winter;

15. A 'London Fog' style trench coat for rain.

Ralph Lauren Polo, Brooks Brothers, LL Bean, and Lands' End offer these items in a predictable range of quality and styles, and a wide variety of price points. Remember the Old Money Order of Things: *Plan*...well in advance. *Earn*...like a man. *Save*...consistently. *Invest*...strategically. *Spend*...wisely. *Plan. Earn. Save. Invest. Spend.*

As you strategize to create or recreate your wardrobe, remember: you are *investing* in yourself. Invest in quality products in traditional styles because they stand the test of time. Keep these helpful hints in mind:

- Take your time; let your style develop;
- Remember and follow the '5% set aside' rule;
- Avoid logos, or keep them small and to a minimum;
- Prioritize your purchasing: acquire items you will wear every day first;
- In terms of quality/price, most of the time you will get what you pay for;
- Look for items that wear well over time, both in terms of style and durability;
- Shop at upscale vintage stores for great deals on high-quality, well-maintained, classic garments.

The Real Thing

A stunning, tasteful, original piece of jewelry is an accessory that enhances a woman's natural beauty. Old Money Gals know that, and keep jewelry to a minimum. Follow their lead: keep the bling to a minimum. Make sure it is appropriate. A little goes a long way. Curate great pieces made with quality materials. Know that counterfeit jewelry or accessories are obvious to the refined eye and should be avoided. I feel very strongly about this for two reasons.

First, counterfeiting name brands is a criminal enterprise. It is lucrative. It is global. It is violent. And it victimizes not just the women who buy the fake items, but also the often abused women who work in hellish conditions for slave wages to produce the merchandise. So, considering this, you can decide if you want to participate in this blood-stained economy in order to impress the easily impressed.

Second, I will tell you that Old Money Gals have razor-sharp radar: they can spot a fake Louis Vuitton bag from across the street. Furthermore, Old Money Gals view the display of counterfeit merchandise as a desperate attempt to impress and as a willingness to deceive. Neither of these is appealing. Neither is tolerated. So, do not come crying to me when you have been dissed and dismissed for owning a piece of counterfeit merchandise.

In the words of the classic Motown hit…ain't nothing like the real thing, baby. An authentic Patek Philippe, Cartier tank watch or stainless steel Rolex says much more than a gaudy display of diamonds or cubic zirconium. Again: Purchase genuine, quality pieces slowly over time. (Unlike counterfeits, they are a wise investment and will last a lifetime.) Extravagant rings, necklaces, and watches have their place. Still, even the most affluent women on the planet opt for discreet luxury when it comes to jewelry to wear on a daily basis.

Piercing and Tattoos

The Old Money Gal is always chic. It should be noted that when she pierces her ears it is only once in each earlobe. I think this is an elegant and refined choice. Piercings in nostrils, eyebrows, and navels often detract from a woman's beauty rather than enhance it, in my opinion.

Not surprisingly, I don't think tattoos are suitable for anyone, especially women. Nevertheless, almost half of Americans between the ages of 18 and 35 have tattoos. Also not surprisingly, almost one quarter of those polled admitted that they regret the decision.

Feel free—for a moment—to discount the fact that I don't like tattoos. Feel free to discount the fact that you're going to spend money on something and get nothing tangible in return. Feel free to discount the fact that many people in decision-making positions do not have a favorable impression of tattoos. (Research confirms this is true.) Feel free to discount the probability that you won't have a favorable impression of your tattoo five years from now. (Research confirms this will be true.) Feel free to discount the fact that Old Money Gals never dream of getting a tattoo. (Trust me on this one.)

Feel free to discount all of the above. Just don't discount your own health. Health? Yes, health. Most women don't give a second thought to the health risks associated with tattoos or, for that matter, 'permanent makeup'. Look at it this way for a moment: prior to having some foreign substance injected into their bodies, many women would, just by way of common sense, visit their physician and get her opinion prior to the procedure. How would this encounter play out? Let's just imagine...

"Good morning," says your doctor, entering the consulting room.

"Good morning," you reply.

"How are you feeling?"

"Fine, thank you." You step right into the subject. "I was thinking about getting a tattoo, and I wanted to know if there were any health issues associated with that."

"Ah,' replies the good doctor, as she leans to a cabinet and pulls out a thick file with the label "Tattoos" on it. She drops the paper brick on the counter with a slap. "Smart decision to come in before rather than after." She's a super-qualified doctor, and she's blunt as a mallet.

"Well, there's the usual stuff I deal with, chronic skin irritations, scarring, infections, and burns. Then there's the toxic ink that's sometimes used, which can affect your immune system and alter pathology specimen interpretations."

You calmly act like you know what 'pathology specimen interpretations' are, but you quickly surmise that 'altering' them is probably not good thing.

"Only 20% of tattoo inks contain carcinogenic compounds," she shrugs, as if she's calculating the odds at a roulette wheel that's playing with your health, not hers. "But those same carcinogens are found in 83% of black ink, which is the most common ink used in tattoos."

"Eeeewwww," you want to whine, but you don't because it takes all your effort just to stop your lip from curling in disgust.

"Those are government statistics, not mine," says Dr. No, as we're now calling her, offhandedly. "The recent studies I've read are finding barium, mercury, copper, and a host of other hazardous chemicals in tattoo ink..."

Your mind is free-associating like a caffeinated lab rat in a maze: the last time you heard the word 'barium' it was followed by the world 'enema'; 'mercury' was followed by 'poisoning'; and 'copper' was followed by...'plumbing', which wasn't so bad, but never mind. Dr. No is still reading from the file and rambling on...

"...What's more, the ingredients *listed* on container labels of tattoo ink and the ingredients actually *found* in the same containers have been determined to be substantially different, frequently. Which is just a wee bit disconcerting..."

Ya think? you want to almost scream.

"The U.S. Food and Drug Administration has recent findings about tattoo ink pigments in which they discovered that many inks are 'industrial grade', that is, suitable for printers and car paint, but not for human beings. Studies are now underway about how these chemicals break down in the body and impact health," she continues, casually scanning more documents in the file.

You try to stop yourself from sinking your chair. "And there are other issues," exhales Dr. No—now a confirmed tattoo party-pooper—"the way metal-based inks increase the likelihood of MRI-induced burns."

Burns?!?

"If you have a medical issue in the future, and I need to request an MRI in order to diagnose something more thoroughly, you may experience a poor reaction because of the metal-based ink tattoos that you've had done. Also, my OBGYN colleagues are finding tattoo ink in biopsy specimens done on lymph nodes, and then there's the Hepatitis C infections, which are ten times more infectious than HIV...transmitted through tattoo needles..."

She's just reading a grocery list now, her eyebrow arching laconically as if to say, 'Oh, I'd forgotten about that miserable possibility.' She pauses to sip some water, then spins back to the file to tell you more, but you've left her office.

Why? Because you've already decided there's no way in hell you're getting a tattoo.

THINGS TO REMEMBER

We've concluded our discussion of Preparation, Comportment, and Clothing and Grooming. These are the three important components of Presentation. Presentation is the manner or style in which something (or someone) is introduced, communicated, or revealed to others. The way you present yourself communicates ideas to others. Know what ideas you're communicating.

Your overall presentation involves Preparation, how well prepared you are for the task or event in front of you; Comportment, how you carry yourself and behave; and your Clothing and Grooming, how you dress and keep yourself. These are areas that, even in the best of women, require constant attention and constant improvement.

Even at a young age, it's important to make the effort to consistently present yourself well. You'll get better results in the world and the habit will contribute to your quality of life. It's going to factor into your overall sense of well-being, as well. As you mature and get to know who you really are, it will be easier to present yourself well. Looking your best and doing your best will be ways that you honor who you are and claim who you want to be.

This journey of discovery is the best way to find the 'look' that is 'you'. You'll lock onto this 'look' more quickly, easily, and less expensively as you refine and embrace your tastes and style, and assess your body and what looks good on you, without regard to passing trends or fads.

Look at photos from your past. Critique your look from a year ago, five years ago, ten years ago. Again, find the look that works for you, own it, preserve it, and think long and hard about changing it.

Presenting yourself well is going to attract a better quality of people into your life. It's also going to impact how they treat you once they are in your life. People are wonderful, but people are human. Most will treat you with respect, but don't tempt the human side by presenting yourself as someone who can be treated casually or with disrespect.

Exemplars – Jackie Kennedy, Katherine Hepburn, and Audrey Hepburn

Three Exemplars close this chapter, each with a unique style, all with grace. Each made significant contributions to our world and to our culture.

Jackie Kennedy—After attending Vassar, the Sorbonne, and George Washington University, Jacqueline Bouvier Kennedy Onassis landed her first job working as a reporter for the *Washington Times-Herald* in 1952. As the paper's "Inquiring Photographer," she roamed the streets of the nation's capital asking strangers their opinions on current topics.

Shortly thereafter, she met and married Jack Kennedy, a senator from Massachusetts. When he was elected President of the United States in 1960, she turned her keen eye for style and design toward overhauling the then-shabby décor of the White House. After burning through her $50,000 budget in a matter of days, she created the Fine Arts Committee for the White House, courted private donors, and went to work acquiring pieces of historically significant furniture from museums and collectors.

She soon transformed the presidential mansion into a more elegant space adorned with tasteful antiques, as well as priceless artifacts once owned by the likes of George Washington and Abraham Lincoln. In 1962, she gave a nationally-televised tour of the renovated White House. The performance won her a special Emmy Award and helped cement her celebrity status.

In 1975, when New York City's Grand Central Terminal train station was dilapidated and in danger of being demolished, she marshaled her considerable resources and saved an architectural and civic treasure.

Today, Jackie—as she will be forever known to millions of women—is widely acknowledged as one of the most stylish women of the 20th century. As an Old Money Gal, she consistently dressed in classic, understated style, and carried herself with dignity and grace, even in the most difficult of circumstances.

"You have to be doing something you enjoy.
That is a definition of happiness."

–Jackie Kennedy

Katherine Hepburn—Born into an Old Money Connecticut family, Katherine Hepburn began acting while enrolled at Bryn Mawr College. Solid reviews for her work on Broadway caught the attention of Hollywood, and off she went to Los Angeles.

Her early years in the film industry were marked with success, including an Academy Award for her third picture, *Morning Glory* (1933). By 1938, however, she'd starred in a series of box office failures and her career languished. Never one to give up, she masterminded her own comeback. Having wisely invested and saved her money, she purchased her own contract back from RKO Radio Pictures then acquired the film rights to *The Philadelphia Story.* She then sold the rights to the studio on the condition that she be the star. (Recognizing the importance of being the master of her own fate, knowing the industry that she worked in, and listening to her own voice, she invested in herself, and her future. Brilliant.)

Three more Oscars came for her work in *Guess Who's Coming to Dinner* (1967), *The Lion in Winter* (1968), and *On Golden Pond* (1981).

Throughout her career and life, she famously shunned the Hollywood social scene and rebuffed its publicity machine. She was intelligent, articulate, outspoken, assertive, athletic, and an independent thinker. She wore pants before it was fashionable for women to do so. With her unconventional lifestyle and unique flair, she was the epitome of the 'modern woman', far ahead of her time.

Look for opportunities to invest in yourself. As you define and refine your own personal style, be inspired by this Old Money Gal. Review photos of Katherine Hepburn. They will serve you well.

"Without discipline, there's no life at all."

–Katharine Hepburn

Audrey Hepburn—Audrey Hepburn became a film star overnight in 1953 after starring with Gregory Peck in *Roman Holiday*. She was the first actress to win an Academy Award, a Golden Globe Award, and a BAFTA Award for a single performance.

Off screen, she was noted for her classic fashion choices and distinctive look. Her influence as a style icon continues even today, decades after the height of her acting career.

She was, however, more than just a pretty face. After the end of the first World War in the 1950s, Audrey narrated two radio programs for UNICEF (the United Nations International Children's Emergency Fund) re-telling children's stories of war, and, in 1989, was appointed a Goodwill Ambassador of UNICEF.

She acted less in later life, living a private life and devoting much of her time to the charity. She was awarded the Presidential Medal of Freedom in recognition of her work with UNICEF as well as the Jean Hersholt Humanitarian Award for her contribution to making the world a better place.

In 2002, at the United Nations Special Session on Children, UNICEF honored her legacy of humanitarian work by unveiling a statue, "The Spirit of Audrey", at UNICEF's New York headquarters.

She is remembered by millions for her radiant smile, indefatigable spirit, and boundless generosity. As you consider these characteristics of an Old Money Gal, learn more about Audrey Hepburn. As you assemble a classic wardrobe, review photos of her.

"Nothing is impossible,
the word itself says 'I'm possible'!"

–Audrey Hepburn

"Police the people in your head."

—Anonymous

May 31, 2017—Sanctuary of the Pilgrims—Sahagan, Spain

CHAPTER 13

Fashion Victims

Old Money Gals are wise to all the attempts made to separate them from their money, to marginalize their worth, or to minimize their opportunities. They don't allow themselves to be victimized by anyone or anything. Ever. Not discrimination, not violence, not outdated social mores.

They aren't victims of these external forces, nor do they victimize themselves.

One aspect of victimization they avoid, and which you'll avoid, is the self-imposed condition of being a 'fashion victim'. Let's look at a few 'fashion victim' categories.

The Basic Fashion Victim: this is the woman who dresses in a way that's too trendy, too provocative, wildly inappropriate, or just plain tasteless, in an attempt to be 'fashionable'. As a result, she looks ridiculous, insecure, clueless, and too easily influenced by passing trends. For example, an older woman who wears a misdemeanor-high miniskirt and low-cut top like she's 18 again can be a fashion victim. A 16 year-old who's trying to dress like a 3-martini-lunch divorcee with high-rise hair and industrial-strength mascara can be a fashion victim.

This faux pas is not really about age, though: it usually occurs when a woman doesn't have a sense of who she is, or has undervalued herself. This sartorial misfire is always cringe-worthy, sometimes humorous, and often sad.

Note: I don't make fun of people who dress in their own unique style or are on the road to refining their style. Other people are not so kind and nonjudgmental. Pay attention, get your thoughts and look together. Avoid being a Basic Fashion Victim. (Remember the words of Coco Chanel, who noted, 'Fashion says, 'Me, too.' Style says, 'Me only.')

By most standards, this type of 'victimization' seems pretty benign. Let me expand on the concept so that you can make better choices and not become a more serious kind of victim.

The Financial Fashion Victim: the woman who is victimized by the excessive prices she pays for clothing and cosmetics. Women pay eye-watering amounts for blouses, pants, skirts, and jackets that often have less fabric and require less work to create when compared to men's garments. While the quality varies from poor to artisan, the mark-up remains the same…staggering. For clothing, this means many women are victimized economically when they need to make a purchase. The Old Money Gal's solution is to selectively buy quality items made of natural fabrics (wool, cotton, linen, silk). Lean toward traditional, classic styles so that your newer items can be easily mixed and matched with your older items. Shop less. Take care of your garments.

You know that the fashion industry introduces new clothing styles and lines every season (winter, spring, summer, and fall) for a reason. The reason they do this is to get new merchandise in front of you, get you into a retail store or online, and get you to purchase new things on a regular basis. The end goal is to take the money from working women and put it in the pockets of multimillion dollar conglomerates. While these big companies charge you big bucks for their goods, they often pay their workers (often women) a few dollars a day to work in sweatshop conditions overseas to make these clothes.

You can't address every problem in the world—just don't be a part of a problem if it's at all possible. Don't be complicit. Don't be an enabler. Don't be a co-conspirator. Research online and learn about the reputation a retailer has with regards to labor practices and community involvement before you buy. Be wise. Shop informed.

Shop like an Old Money Gal: *when you need to*, not when you're feeling depressed, not when you're feeling happy, not because you want to 'treat' others, not when you're feeling powerful, not when you're feeling unattractive, not when you're having relationship problems, not when you're feeling worried, not when you just got a pay raise or promotion, and not when you're simply feeling bored.

Note: be the best global citizen you can be. Know your vendors. Be the savvy, financially independent woman. Invest in yourself. Acquire the best. Save money at every opportunity, both as a sound financial practice and as you shop. No shopping sprees and no credit card purchases. Budget, budget, budget.

Saving Face

The Health Fashion Victim refers to the woman who is victimized by the toxins found in the beauty products she buys and uses. This issue is an enormous one, given the size of the cosmetics industry in the United States. (Recent statistics suggest that American women outspend women in every other country in the world on beauty products.)

As with everything you purchase, it's important to know the 'true costs' of owning and using a product. For example, if you buy a yacht, you not only have to pay for the vessel. You must pay for insurance, maintenance, fuel, crew, and a place to dock it. The same issues apply to the acquisition of an exotic car, a serious fur coat, or piece of jewelry. Steep as they can be, the 'true costs' of these purchases are only financial.

With beauty products, we're talking about your most prized possession: your health. So, I'm going to specifically address some of the toxins found in cosmetics sold in the United States in hopes that you become more aware about the 'true costs' of some of the choices you make when you purchase beauty products.

Again, these are the costs you pay, not just with the 'purchase price' of the product, but the price you pay with your health. According to recent reports, European authorities have banned 1,373 substances from cosmetics sold to European women. The United States Food and Drug Administration has, by contrast, banned only 8 and restricted only 3. (Think about that.) Researchers have linked some of these chemicals to various health issues due to their known or suspected effects on hormones in the human body.

The question you may want to ask yourself is this: if European government officials have banned this many substances from the cosmetics that can be sold to their citizens—most of whom are women and young girls—shouldn't you care enough about yourself and your daughters to investigate, become informed, and ban these same toxins from your life?

Before I discuss in detail the hazards associated with many cosmetics on the market today in the United States, I want to discuss makeup's health effects on our young women and girls. I'll refer to 'tweens'—girls between the ages of 10 and 12—and teenagers first.

It's important to be aware that more teens and tweens are wearing makeup than at any other time in history. Sadly, today's American teens and tweens have been brainwashed to believe that they have an 'image' to create and maintain. For many, that image includes masking their faces in makeup every day. Many of them absolutely refuse to leave home without it.

Many teenagers in North America have a daily makeup ritual that includes lipstick, powder, blush, foundation, mascara, eyeliner, nail polish, and perfume, not to mention skin lotion, shampoo, conditioner, and hair color treatments. In fact, experts estimate that a typical young girl now walks around with at least a dozen beauty products on her body. As the makeup layers add up, so does her exposure to dangerous chemicals, and that's very bad news for a young girl's health.

Two specific types of chemicals known as parabens and phthalates are found in many cosmetics and have been found to disrupt hormone levels. Since teens tend to use makeup more often, for longer periods of time, and more heavily than adults, they have a greater chance of suffering from health and skin problems early in life as a result of constant exposure to these toxins.

Additionally, peer pressure can often prompt them to cover any blemishes with *even more* makeup. In turn, this action brings on or worsens acne, creating a harmful cycle of skin damage that may take months or years to reverse. It is truly a vicious cycle.

Will makeup change the way skin appears? Absolutely. Teens and tweens might have a skewed idea of the immediate effect makeup has on their skin, but they may not fully comprehend the problematic correlation it has to skin problems. A recent study in Brazil revealed that 45 percent of women who used makeup religiously had skin diseases related to the makeup they were wearing.

Makeup can wreak havoc, inflicting damaging and lasting effects on a teenager's skin. As previously stated, the European Union has banned over 1300 substances from cosmetics sold to European women and girls. Most of the makeup products on the market in the United States actually have some of these 1300 harmful chemicals in them. Again: researchers have linked these chemicals to various health issues due to the known or suspected effects on hormones. (Think about that.)

Collateral Damage

I think of puberty as a *special delight*—in retrospect, and for other people. It's a twisting tunnel of change, an emotional roller coaster. Unexpected growth spurts and new, intoxicating emotions keep adolescents who are barely in control of their maturing bodies constantly on edge. All anyone can do is hang on and try to make it through relatively unscathed.

It is a tricky process: you have no warning when it will start, what the ride will be like, and most importantly, when it will end. The young bodies of teens and tweens neck deep in puberty are changing at lightning speed. Luckily, the human body is naturally equipped to handle this turbulent transition. However, many of the chemicals used in makeup can dangerously and unpredictably offset the young body's organic balancing act during this period.

What's more, the *manner* in which tweens and teens use makeup adds to the health risks. As adult women, you may share your makeup with your 'girls' (a little blush here, a touch of mascara, a little extra liner pencil, and just a dab of lip gloss). Generally, though, you carry your makeup. Your friends carry theirs. You know what you're using. It's not a 'pass around pack'.

However, teens and tweens generally have a much larger circle of friends with whom they share makeup. For the most part they have no idea of how those friends (with whom they are sharing their makeup) are using their own makeup, or who *they* are sharing it with. Why is this a hazard?

Liquids like primer, foundation, lip gloss, mascara, and their applicator brushes provide a fertile breeding ground for bacteria. Unwitting users then add their own bacteria cocktail from their lips, hands, eyes, and faces. That bottle, tube, applicator brush, or sponge then turns the makeup into a dangerous culprit for a whole host of illnesses and diseases. Unknowingly, teens and tweens often spread harmful bacteria exponentially through shared makeup products. As we discussed, makeup can have annoying and damaging effects on its users, especially developing teens and tweens. Already dealing with skin issues from raging hormones, genes, and germs in the environment around them, the last thing they need are additional makeup-related health issues.

Symptoms like pink eye, staph infections, and those awful makeup-induced acne lesions, medically known as 'acne-cosmetica', can be a result of wearing makeup too soon, too frequently, and too heavily. We all know that teen acne is no laughing matter: for teens and tweens in an often brutal peer pressure environment, it can make the problems of puberty a thousand times worse. Taking a step back, reassessing the role of beauty products in your life, and defining a new, common-sense approach are key.

The Simple Solution

Many of the known side effects associated with teens and tweens using makeup can be simply and easily resolved. It is your responsibility to create a proper skin care routine—for yourself and your daughters—early in order to develop and maintain beautiful skin naturally. I would suggest that young girls under the age of 16 not wear any makeup at all. When teens do begin to wear makeup, they should take care to use water-based makeup and apply it sparingly with clean brushes.

It is your responsibility to find products free from harmful chemicals that will support a healthy makeup collection. When in doubt about a product or ingredient, do your own research before applying it to your skin.

One great resource is the Skin Deep Cosmetic Safety Database – which you can access at *CosmeticsDatabase.com.* Just plug in the name of your favorite makeup product and the database will tell you if it contains any known dangerous ingredients.

Again: you must also ask yourself if you know exactly what you're purchasing—the product, and its 'true costs' to you and your health—when you buy cosmetics. You're not just getting the benefit of 'the look' they provide. You're getting the impact—short and long term—of the health risks they carry. You should also ask yourself this: 'Even if I adopt a devil-may-care attitude toward my own health and my own life with regards to cosmetics, what health risks am I exposing my children—born and unborn—to?'

When toxins get into your bloodstream, they don't just stay with you. You pass them on to your child before they're born, and afterward, during the breastfeeding process. Furthermore, if you set an example of purchasing and using toxic cosmetics on yourself, can you blame your daughters for adopting your habits, buying the same toxic products, and using them? Is that really a legacy you want to pass on?

I will tell you this about Old Money Gals: when it comes to their health and the health of their children, they ask a lot of hard questions, and they continue to ask hard questions until they get satisfactory answers. If they don't get a satisfactory answer about a product that may affect their health or the health of their family, it's over: they don't buy the product. They don't allow it in the house. They don't allow their children to use it. They prioritize health over appearance because nothing is more beautiful than a woman with healthy, clean, fresh skin.

Police the people in your head, especially the ones telling you that you must wear makeup to be attractive. Listen to your instincts. Listen to your body. Know that the 'true cost' of 'beauty' can never be at the expense of your health.

Toxic Relationships

Now, let's take a look at some of the ingredients in cosmetics that victimize women and girls, and the health problems they cause. These substances include:

- Parabens—these chemicals have been found to disrupt hormonal levels as they mimic the hormone estrogen and are linked to cancer, reproductive toxicity, immunotoxicity, neurotoxicity, and skin irritation, as well as increasing the chances of breast cancer. They are found in shampoos and other bath products.
- Formaldehyde—found in nail polish and hair treatments, a known carcinogen.
- 'Fragrance'—this word on a product label can mean anything, as companies aren't required to disclose what chemicals are included. Common toxins include hormone disruptors which contribute to breast cancer,

among other things. Avoid this by purchasing products scented only with organic essential oils.

- Coal Tar Dyes—banned from food products, but still found in hair dyes, lipsticks, and other products. Look for the 'color index' (CI), followed by a 5 digit number on the ingredients label to determine if Coal Tar Dyes are present in a product.
- Talc—found in eye shadows, body powders, face powders, and many loose mineral products. Contributes to ovarian tumors, among other things.
- Mineral oil—a petroleum-based product and a known carcinogen. Found in baby lotions, creams, and lip balms, among other things.
- Aluminum zirconium—found in antiperspirants and linked to the development of Alzheimer's disease, as well as breast cancer.
- Sodium laureth—found in a variety of cosmetics, causing skin damage, eye damage, and liver damage. One of the most dangerous unregulated products found in a variety of beauty products (shower gel, exfoliant, liquid hand soap, and toothpaste). Has long been used in industrial cleaning products.
- BHA and BHT (Butylated Hydroxyanisole & Butylated Hydroxytoluene)—preservatives widely used by the food industry, also found in a range of cosmetics, these damage the reproductive system and impede proper thyroid function, among other things.

There is an extreme injustice in the fact that many women voluntarily pay exorbitant prices for cosmetics that, first, enrich male-dominated companies, and, second, contribute to a wide range of illnesses, many of them deadly to women. It is easy to avoid being a fashion victim, both in terms of health and finances, when it comes to cosmetics: become informed, purchase healthier, and purchase less.

Exemplar – Shirley Chisholm

Shirley Chisholm was born on November 30, 1924, in Brooklyn, New York, but spent her formative years in Barbados with her grandmother. After graduating from Brooklyn College, she began her career as a teacher and then earned a master's degree from Columbia University.

During her years as a teacher, Ms. Chisholm began volunteering with the League of Women Voters and the Seventeenth Assembly District Democratic Club. In 1964, she ran for and was elected to the New York State Assembly.

Ms. Chisholm was a member of the assembly from 1965 to 1968, where, among other things, she worked to get unemployment benefits extended to domestic workers. She also sponsored the introduction of the SEEK program (Search for Education, Elevation and Knowledge) which gave the state's underprivileged students the chance to enter college while receiving intensive remedial education. She sponsored another bill which prohibited female teachers from losing tenure while out on maternity leave.

In 1968, when she ran for and was elected to the U.S. Congress, where she served on several House committees including Agriculture, Veterans' Affairs, Rules and Education, and Labor.

During the height of the civil rights movement, she spoke out about the judicial system, police brutality, prison reform, gun control, and drug abuse, issues which we still struggle with today.

Throughout her terms in Congress, she met with discrimination, both for being black and for being a woman. Still, when George Wallace, an outspoken opponent of integration and equal rights for blacks, was shot and wounded during his presidential campaign, Ms. Chisholm went to visit him in the hospital. She showed compassion for a fellow human being, even if his political beliefs were different than hers.

Seeking to have an even greater influence on society, Ms. Chisholm ran for the office of the President of the United States of America in 1972. Although she did not win the Democratic nomination, she did win an impressive 10 percent of the votes within her party.

She served in the U.S. House of Representatives for another decade, retiring in 1982. After leaving Congress, Ms. Chisholm made her home in suburban Williamsville, New York and resumed her career in education. She was named to the Purington Chair at the all-women Mount Holyoke College in Massachusetts.

She also co-founded the Unity Democratic Club in Brooklyn and was one of the early members of the National Organization for Women (NOW) as well as being active in the National Association for the Advancement of Colored People (NAACP). She was inducted into the National Women's Hall of Fame in 1993.

"Unbought and Unbossed" was her campaign slogan, and she stayed that way all through her life and career.

"If they don't give you a seat at the table, bring a folding chair."

–Shirley Chisholm

"Eventually you must pay for what you purchase."

—Anonymous

May 2, 2017—Geneva, Switzerland

CHAPTER 14

It's Always Personal

Personal finance can be defined as the manner in which a woman addresses the acquisition, management, preservation, and growth of money and things of value that she personally has access to, receives, or controls. In addition to what are traditionally termed 'assets', this also refers to debts, liabilities, and issues of taxation. We're going to compartmentalize these in terms of acquisition (earning through employment and entrepreneurship, as well as inheritance and windfalls), management (expenditures), and preservation and growth (saving and investing).

Note: I do not give investment advice about which stocks, bonds, or financial instruments to purchase. Likewise, I will not advise on the acquisition of real estate, precious metals, or any other investment class. I will, however, offer thoughts on how to think about investing, which is very different.

How these issues of acquisition, management, and preservation and growth are considered is a very individual process: how you approach them will depend greatly on your own financial situation, your personal situation, and your goals. As an example, the approach to personal finance for a 22 year-old college student with a trust fund and a 40 year-old working mother of two on a salary are going to be different. How they'll look at employment, consider investing, and prioritize spending may be worlds apart. However, the fundamentals presented here remain constant.

As we begin our discussion of personal finance, we must acknowledge that it does not happen in a vacuum. Social and political factors influence a woman's ability to make, keep, and grow her nest egg. There exists an unjust and unfair landscape that women face in this area, which is often reflected in statistics. For example, while women control over 80% of the decisions made regarding consumer spending, they earn 20 to 45% less than their male counterparts in the workplace. Reports vary country to country around the world, but the reality remains: women purchase for themselves and their family members—what some economists refer to as 'circle spending', i.e., buying decisions made for their 'family circle'—yet they remain underpaid.

Despite arguably doing more of the work (at home and the office) and being paid less (on the job, not to mention getting zero pay at home), women around the world still manage to control billions in assets. Day in and day out, they make economic decisions which multinational corporations rely upon for their very existence, not to mention their profits. Day in and day out, women often balance the budget and the checkbook for their families and monitor savings and investment as well.

As the gatekeepers of what does and does not enter the family home, a woman's choices are pivotal. If a woman decides a product or service is unsafe—for them or their families—the product or service will not sell. It is doomed. Just as we've said that you must pay for what you purchase, corporations will also pay for making products that do not resonate with women, are not considerate of women, or that are not approved of by women. Be attentive to the power you as a woman have.

Again, women are the economic 'final arbiters' of much of what their children, husbands, and families buy, do, participate in, or avoid. The opinions and choices of women around the world factor heavily into almost every economic indicator or forecast currently in use. Women as a group are the single largest influence on an economy, whether it's a good influence like savings and investment rates, or a bad influence like consumer debt.

At this point in the 21st century, women enjoy more rights, privileges, and opportunities than at other time in history. Gone are the days when women were completely dependent on men for information, opportunity, protection and survival. Women now have the option to work outside the home, start a business, own property, influence the economy, and gain or retain any level of financial independence they choose.

This fresh, new generation of women is stepping into entrepreneurship, embracing and driving innovation. As they do, a new wave of businesses with women-centered values and ideas is emerging. These businesses more accurately address women's needs, desires, and pain points. These businesses are more likely to be sustainable, organic, cruelty free, and toxin free.

Historically overlooked and underfunded in venture capital circles, women are now in financial positions of power. Most women know that 80% of the products they purchase are designed, built, and sold to women by men. They also know that this can, and must, change.

Remember: all you need is a vision, a commitment to hard work, access to some resources, and a little bit of luck. You may not make a million dollars, but you could make two, five, or ten million. Saved and invested wisely, proceeds from your job or business can provide you with options. And options are one of the most important things you can have in life. Don't sit and wait for opportunities to improve your financial situation. Rise up and create them for yourself. Forget 'leveling the playing field'. Today's 'playing fields' have been created by men and are coded for men. Create your own. Think entrepreneurship.

I'm sharing all of this with you prior to a discussion of 'personal finance' in order to alter your perception of yourself. As I mentioned in the Introduction, you are the one who earns, manages, spends, and invests your money. You may be at a disadvantage in some instances, but you are not a victim. You are not helpless. You are in the driver's seat. Make no mistake about it: in a capitalist society, money is power. While you may be reading this and be under a mountain of credit card or student debt, you can turn your situation around with the application of some personal finance fundamentals. All it takes is some awareness, some choices, and some time.

Throughout these chapters, I'm going to ask you to constantly remember the Old Money Order of Things when it comes to personal finance: Plan. Earn. Save. Invest. Spend. Emblazon these words upon your retina. Each step is important, and the order of each step is important. One step at a time.

'I 'will' what I want.

—Anonymous

Declarations of Independence

Let's get a handle on the often-discussed concept of 'financial independence'. It means different things to different people, but there are some common benchmarks that we can establish. These benchmarks will help you understand where you are presently and chart where you want to be in the future. These benchmarks have corresponding levels of 'independence'—options or choices you do or don't have.

When you see 'financial independence' in these terms, you will be more inclined to make choices with your money because money will become not something you use to purchase *things*, but a tool you use purchase your *freedom*. Here are the three basic, broad categories of financial independence and the freedoms associated with each:

Minimum Independence: If you only have enough money to make it through the end of the month, your independence is *limited*: you have to go to work, even at a job you don't like. The people you work with may be jerks and the work you're assigned awful or boring, but you feel obligated because you have to honor your commitments and pay your bills. In this situation, you may not fulfill your potential and end up feeling less than fantastic about yourself.

Intermediate Independence: If you have enough money in savings to pay the rent and eat beans for 6 months to a year, you have *more freedom*, especially if you get laid off or want to start a business in your living room. If someone mistreats you at work, you can stand up to them confidently, litigate, and/or leave. You can seek and wait for a job you really like. You can take a job that doesn't pay all that well, for a period of time, knowing that you have a pad of cash to cushion you as you move forward to your goal.

Optimum Independence: If you have enough money to live the rest of your life without working for a paycheck, you have a *maximum amount* of freedom, a multitude of options. Ironically, to be happy, most of the options you'll consider will involve work. The big difference is that you get to choose the work you do, and it will probably be the work you love to do.

You can probably imagine or have experienced first-hand the Minimum and

Intermediate stages of financial independence. It may be helpful, though, to get a picture of the Optimum. So let's do that quickly.

As a woman of independent means, you have the opportunity to do work that is rewarding—personally and financially. When you find this, *you at work* will resemble a *child at play.* You will wake up excitedly looking forward to your day and eagerly anticipating all that it holds. You're ready to do your work joyfully and, when the end of the day comes, you will only reluctantly set it aside to get some rest and get something to eat. It may or may not make money, but you will be living and working 'on purpose' as psychologists say. And it will feel good.

This describes the daily life of a woman who is financially independent. She has a purpose in her life, which she actively works at. She has her spending under control. She has her investments working for her, providing an income she can live on. This is 'passive income', a concept we'll discuss in more detail later. This is true freedom. This is the target to aim for.

Note: if you see a woman who has a great deal of money at her disposal, but she's never satisfied with the amount of material possessions she has, she is actually impoverished: she constantly needs exterior reinforcement—a new purchase—to feel good about herself. Don't envy her. She's suffering. So forget her. Let's focus now on the Old Money Gal's financial priorities: financial freedom through the acquisition of money and things of value, the management of your money, and the preservation and growth of your wealth.

'It always seems impossible until it is done.'

—Nelson Mandela

Exemplar – Mary Anning

Born in 1799, Mary Anning overcame the lack a formal education to emerge as one of the greatest fossil pioneers and one of the world's foremost authorities on paleontology. In order to read works of Georges Cuvier, the eminent naturalist and paleontologist, she taught herself French.

In 1821, Ms. Anning found three fossilized ichthyosaur skeletons, ranging from

5 to 20 feet long. Ms. Anning was now working at the forefront of a new science utilizing fossils to better understand the earth's natural history.

Collector George Cumberland described Ms. Anning's 5 foot ichthyosaur this way: "the very finest specimen of a fossil Ichthyosaurus ever found in Europe… we owe entirely to the persevering industry of a young female fossilist, of the name of Anning… and her dangerous employment. To her exertions we owe nearly all the fine specimens of Ichthyosauri of the great collections…"

At the tender age of 24, Ms. Anning made the first discovery and drawing of a complete Plesiosaurus skeleton. The discovery was so incredible that many scientists refused to believe such a creature had ever existed.

Initially declaring the find a fake, Georges Cuvier later changed his tune after carefully examining the fossilized findings and declared: "It is the most amazing creature ever discovered".

The discovery of Plesiosaurus secured Ms. Anning's reputation. Nevertheless she continued to work relentlessly. In 1828, she discovered the *'Ink bag of Belemnoidea'* fossils, ten-armed creatures that could eject ink into the water, like squid. Remarkably, Ms. Anning found that the ink in the bags had survived fossilization and could still be used in pens. Paying homage to her, artists in her hometown began using Belemnoidea ink to draw pictures of fossils found in the area.

Ms. Anning also found examples of fossilized animal feces, and, breaking some open, found bones and fish scales inside. This discovery gave scientists a window into the diets of animals that lived hundreds of millions of years ago.

In 1829, Ms. Anning found a second Plesiosaur fossil, even more complete than her groundbreaking discovery of 1823. In 1830, Ms. Anning discovered one of her most complete and beautiful fossilized creatures – Plesiosaurus macrocephalus, a cast of which is on display at the Natural History Museum in Paris, France.

While her discoveries formed the basis of much of our early understanding of prehistoric animal life, and her advice directed much of the work done by her contemporaries in the field, she hardly received her due during her lifetime.

Her contributions were eventually recognized: almost 200 years after her death, the Royal Society published a roster of the ten British women who most influenced science, and Mary Anning's name was on the list.

> *"Mary Anning is probably the most important unsung (or inadequately sung) collecting force in the history of paleontology."*
>
> —Stephen Jay Gould

"Math has no opinion."

—Cathy O'Neil

August 18, 2018—The Dance of Triumph—Paris, France

CHAPTER 15

Mergers and Acquisitions

Now, let's talk about you: how to get you—and keep you—financially independent or wealthy, doing what you love to do, what you're good at, and what you were put on this earth to do. (If you're lucky, you know what they are and they're the same thing.)

Your first step is to maximize the 'merger' of your education, credentials, experience, and skills in order to market yourself and your abilities. You merge these to the best of your ability in order to make the 'acquisition' of money easier and to make the possibility of making more money in the future more likely.

Many times, at the start of this quest, you interview for and are offered a job. At this point, you may experience the pervasive gender gap that women around the world face every day. According to a 2017 report from the National Partnership for Women and Families, women of color earn 25-40% less than their white male counterparts. Caucasian women fair a little better, but the difference in pay for women when compared to men remains a serious problem.

The reality today is that women work longer hours to make the same pay as men. Women also do more 'unpaid labor': taking care of husbands, children, in-laws, and parents. I don't know of any statistics that support this assertion. It's just something I've seen my entire life, and it's an experience that has never been denied by anyone—male or female—that I've spoken to in my entire life.

I'm uncertain about how to change family dynamics, but you as a woman can definitely change workplace dynamics. Go to your library, and your librarian, and find books and resources to help you negotiate more effectively for equal pay when you are offered a job or seek a promotion. You'll also find resources online, but talk to other women (and men) when possible. Human interaction gives you the best chance to receive inside information that isn't found in search results. It offers the opportunity to speak with someone who may become a mentor, ally, colleague, or friend.

However, the truth is that the responsibility for earning and acquiring money rests mostly with you. To maximize your earning potential, consider the following:

- Think like an entrepreneur, even if you work for a company;
- Be willing to do the jobs your peers don't want to do;
- Search for a 'niche market' i.e., an under-serviced or specialty area within your chosen field that you can focus on, dominate, and be 'the expert' in;
- Be willing to relocate—even to another country—if there are opportunities to earn more, do more, and be more;
- Know your 'pain centers'—points of dissatisfaction or discomfort—that motivate you and use them to find solutions that can be profitable to you and others;
- Master the fundamentals of your chosen field and obtain any necessary certifications or training so you can always earn money and take care of yourself.

In your current work position:

- Be a problem solver for your company, as problem solvers are 'golden nuggets' for business owners who always face a myriad of daily challenges;
- Come in a little early, leave a little later, and do a little more;
- Consistently go 'above and beyond' what your job requires as you look for opportunities to learn more;
- As you do, keep a detailed list of the extra responsibilities you've voluntarily taken on, or have been given;
- Consistently calendar your performance, so you can document—for yourself and your boss—that you're doing these extra tasks on a regular basis;
- After a period of time (6 months or so) of day in, day out competent performance of your assigned duties and handling of the 'above and beyond' responsibilities you've taken on, set at appointment to talk with your boss;
- Detail your performance modestly but evenly, and politely ask for a raise;
- If you are given a raise, thank your boss and continue to do all of your work;
- If you are not, assess the reasons given for the refusal;
- Begin a concerted effort to look for a new job;
- Always be the hardest worker in the room;
- Do not settle.

WILL POWER

Another way that you may acquire money or things of value is through a windfall or an inheritance. A windfall may be a winning lottery ticket (don't bet on it), or a settlement from litigation in a civil case. An inheritance is far more likely. I've discussed this important issue in *The Old Money Book*, and I suggest you read about it there. Nevertheless, I'll cover it briefly here, as it presents an incredible opportunity to improve your life and move you toward financial independence.

Let's say that you're invited to a lawyer's office for an important meeting. *Dear me, what could this be about?* Well, as it happens, your Uncle Chester has kicked the bucket. And? And...there's the issue of the will. You throw on a respectable ensemble, give your hair a lick and a promise, and take the train into the city. Shortly thereafter, you're sitting in a wood-paneled conference room that's larger than your apartment. The courtly, aging lawyer is straight out of a Charles Dickens novel. In short order, he informs you that Uncle Chester, the old codger who lived in a two room cottage in Vermont, had actually socked away a tidy sum...and he's left it all to you.

Gulp. As the blood returns to your head, Uncle Chester's lawyer congratulates you in that very *Great Expectations* kind of way and asks you to sign on the dotted line. He then asks where you'd like to have the funds deposited, and wishes you the best of luck. At this point in time, you don't need luck: you need to manage that money wisely. So, my suggestion would be to immediately contact a reputable certified public accountant (CPA) and assess any tax liability that the inheritance may present to you. (Pay your taxes fully and promptly. You want no issues with your Uncle Sam.)

The second thing you might want to do is buy a bottle of champagne and toast your good fortune. Alone. As I strongly suggest in *The Old Money Book*, I would keep the inheritance a secret. Note that a 'secret' is not something you tell one person at a time. You don't need your inheritance affecting your relationships. Deal with the change privately. Then, later, decide how to share it with others, if at all.

Don't do anything different with your daily routine or your life. Don't quit your job, even if you don't like your boss. Don't purchase anything. Instead, make a list of everything you *could purchase and do*. Travel, paying off debt, new car, bigger apartment, fur coat, limousine rides for you and your friends, and shoes, shoes, shoes. Call that the Crazy List. The list with things on it that, once you hand over your money, you get nothing of value in return. That's crazy, right?

Now make a Smart List. This is a list of everything you *could invest in*. This list is everything you could put money in that would, once you hand over your money, increase in value and pay you back over time. Start the list with income-producing real estate, dividend-paying stocks, annuities, tax-free bonds...things that produce that 'passive income' we spoke of earlier in the book. No, it's not as much fun as renting a limousine, but it is more rewarding in the long run. You might also consider investing in yourself with education.

I'm not telling you what to invest in. I'm not telling you to invest. I am telling you not to spend. And only consider investing after a 'cooling off period' of 3 to 6 months *after you inherit the money*. Again: as the euphoria wears off, brew a cup of hot tea, curl up on the sofa, and assess how much this inheritance can help you achieve your goal of being financially independent. If you spend it all in a week, it doesn't help you at all. If you spend it all in two years, it may help you a little. If you invest it and make it work for you—and pay you dividends or interest every month—it may benefit you for the rest of your life.

Consider the amount you've inherited, how you can best use it, and look at where you are. Is this going to give you Intermediate Independence? Optimum Independence? View this inheritance not as money, but as an opportunity. Then use it wisely. As you know, math has no opinion. Do the math when you get an inheritance. Make it work for you in the long term.

Things To Remember

The more initiative you take in assessing, refining, and using your talents to move yourself forward, the better you're going to feel about yourself.

Don't worry that you can't 'control' everything. You can control what you're thinking and what you're doing. If you find yourself thinking negative thoughts, steer your mind back down a more constructive path. If you're wasting time or doing something that's self-destructive or less than helpful to your future, retreat from it.

You as a woman are not a 'special interest group'. You are not the 'exception to the rule'. You are the rule. So rule. Don't allow yourself to be marginalized by the assumptions of others.

So, to summarize, you're going to do everything you can with regards to training, preparation, innovation, vision, and hard work to legally and ethically earn and acquire as much money as you can. As you do, the next aspect of your finances will be how you manage what you earn.

Exemplar – Wangari Maathai

Wangari Maathai was born in 1940 in Nyeri, a rural region in Kenya, Africa. She came to the United States as a student, obtaining degrees from Mount St. Scholastica College in Atchison, Kansas, and from the University of Pittsburgh. She then pursued her doctorate studies in Germany and at the University of Nairobi. Awarded a Ph.D. in 1971 from the University of Nairobi, she was the first woman from East and Central Africa to earn a doctorate degree. She also taught veterinary medicine at the university.

In addition to her academic accomplishments, Professor Maathai was instrumental in the establishment of the Green Belt Movement. The community-based organization focuses on planting trees in order to reduce poverty and promote conservation efforts in Africa.

She also became involved in politics, representing the Tetu constituency in Kenya's parliament from 2002 to 2007. She was awarded a Nobel Peace Prize Laureate in 2004 for her work, and served as Assistant Minister for Environment and Natural Resources in Kenya's ninth parliament. In 2005, she was appointed Goodwill Ambassador to the Congo Basin Forest Ecosystem by the eleven Heads of State in the Congo region.

In 2007, Professor Maathai was invited to be co-chair of the Congo Basin Fund, an initiative established by the British and the Norwegian governments to help protect the Congo forests. In 2010, she became a trustee of the Karura Forest Environmental Education Trust, which was established to safeguard public land.

Professor Maathai was internationally recognized for her efforts to promote democracy, human rights, and environmental conservation. Despite her busy schedule, she also found time to write. She authored four books: *The Green Belt Movement; Unbowed: A Memoir; The Challenge for Africa;* and *Replenishing the Earth.*

"It's the little things citizens do. That's what will make the difference. My little thing is planting trees."

—Wangari Maathai

"Experience is the hardest kind of teacher. It gives you the test first and the lesson afterwards."

—Oscar Wilde

May 28, 2017—San Juan de Ortega, Spain

CHAPTER 16

You'll Manage

As you progress in your career with a company or your own business, the flow of money will increase. As it does, you'll have the opportunity to move yourself up the ladder in terms of financial independence. This is where money management comes into the picture. Keep in mind that it's not just about money. It's about independence and quality of life, of which money is an important part.

At the outset, your immediate goal will be to accumulate your 'emergency fund' that will cover all your living expenses for 6 months to one year without additional income or work. You will save consistently in order to assemble this fund, in cash, in the bank. It will sit there, and is only to be used for an *emergency*. In this context, an emergency is a situation in which you are not able to generate an income due to illness or unemployment. It will provide you with necessary funds to recover your health or find a new job. It is not for a new purse, a new car, or a vacation.

Only after you have this fund in place will you begin to consider investing. You will leave your emergency fund untouched and invest with money you save over and above that emergency fund amount.

Old Money Management

Cicero once said that well-managed money is like a second source of income. Think about that for a minute. I know librarians who live as well as fashion models earning three times the annual income. How do those crazy librarians do it? By managing their money well and living simply.

Similarly, Old Money Gals have learned the discipline and art of streamlining their expenditures. They have taken a hard look at where their money goes and if it's really going to something that's 'essential'. If it isn't, they cut it out of the budget or find a more economical alternative. They've established priorities:

- the first is to be healthy (eat well and exercise);
- the second is to spend quality time and have meaningful engagement with the people they love (family and friends);
- the third is to do work they love;
- the fourth is to live within their means (earn more than they spend);
- the fifth is to remain or become financially independent.

Following these priorities, they manage their purchases using a matrix of their income, the importance of the purchase, and the value of that purchase over time.

Expensive Expenses

Income is initially impacted by your true, necessary, non-negotiable expenses: rent, food, and the basics for clothing. You may then add medical insurance, car expenses, phone, electric, and heating costs (utilities). As you add up your true baseline costs for living, you deduct those from your income and are left with your 'disposable income'. Then, you have 'optional expenses.' Be realistic here. If you're going to have a bottle of wine every week and that's 'your thing', then budget that in. Don't lie to yourself about your necessities and optional expenses, including personal care expenses like manicures, pedicures, hair care, and entertainment.

You will, however, be required to assess the importance of all expenses that impact your amount of disposable income. You'll determine if those expenses are worth the price of not achieving financial independence as quickly as you'd like (expenses like going to restaurants, nightclubs, and shopping randomly online).

What Old Money Gals do is start by asking themselves a question: what am I going to use every day? I'm going to use food, dishes, pots and pans in the kitchen. I'm going to sleep on a bed every night. I'm going to sit in a chair or on a sofa every day. I may need a car to get to work five days a week. So that's that: you need those things you use every day. (In case you missed it, *The Old Money Book* discusses how to acquire furniture economically, refurbish it tastefully, and have it last a lifetime, among other things.)

Another category of things you need is clothes. Here, again, the 'what am I going to use every day?' question arises. You are going to purchase the clothes you wear every day first. An evening dress or a fur coat is going to be farther down the list... if they're on the list at all. If you can purchase something that can be used for work and leisure, that's better: you get double the use. So ask yourself: how versatile is it?

You must control impulse purchases. Take a moment. Purchase the item 'in your head' first. 'Own' it for a minute. Then 'put it back on the shelf'. Two days later, if you still think it's a good value—and something you're going to use almost every day—then consider the purchase again. If you can't pay cash for it, don't buy it.

Remember again the Old Money Order of Things: *Plan. Earn. Save. Invest. Spend.* Again, key points to review as you consider a purchase:

- First, the price...which is the cash price, the 'credit price' (what you'll pay in interest if you don't pay it off at the end of the month) and the 'waste price', what it will cost you in terms of other opportunities that you could not take advantage of because you wasted money on this purchase;
- Second, your disposable income;
- Third, the importance of the item;
- Fourth, the true value of the item over time.

This 'true value of the item over time' refers to how well the product is going to perform by comparing the expense of the item (the price) to the duration (expected lifetime) of its use and benefit, including how often you're going to use it and how necessary it is. To use a math metaphor: the price of an item divided by its lifespan equals its 'true value'.

We have to pull all of these strategies and all this advice back to the 'Big Picture'. That 'Big Picture' is you being financially independent as soon as possible through proper money management. It's your responsibility. Start today.

~ OLD MONEY SECRET ~

In order to maximize opportunities and enjoy any security in life, solid money management is critical. A personal budget and savings plan must be in place and adhered to. Awareness about the amount of money being spent, and why, is key. An investment strategy is implemented and results closely monitored. 'Wealth' is viewed as the ability to enjoy independence and quality of life, not the ability to purchase things.

* * * * * * * *

Break Up and Break Out

Now, let's look at the Spending part of Management. Spending all the money you earn doesn't help you. It makes progress difficult, if not impossible. So let's take a long, hard look at what makes it difficult, if not impossible, for so many women to save money.

Women today face the realities of student debt, limited employment prospects, as well as the gender wage gap we've already discussed. Throw in the rising costs of food and housing, and it's a real party. I can't do anything about the economy, and you may not be able to, either.

There are personal expenses and habits, however, that you can 'break up with' in order to help yourself 'break out' and make financial progress more quickly and more efficiently. There are things that may be hurting your efforts to be financially independent. In this section on Spending, we're going to itemize those in order to effectively address them.

At some point in your life, you've broken up with someone and ended a relationship, or someone has broken up with you. The scenario is at least awkward and at most excruciatingly painful. We try to tell ourselves that it's for the best, and sometimes it is. But it can still be unpleasant. Likewise, let me again suggest this: it's going to be best for your financial well-being if you 'break up' with some of the products, services, and habits you've adopted. It may be painful, but in the long run, you'll be better off.

Here are some 'financial break ups' I encourage, starting from the simplest and easiest…to the most complicated and difficult. Consider the following Easy Break Ups:

- Break up with all the 'stuff'—clothing, furniture, dishes, trinkets, etc.—that you aren't using. Sell it or give it away. The extra money you make from the sales will come in handy. The good you'll do by giving to charity will help others and make you feel better;
- Break up with the 'new phone syndrome'. Don't upgrade your phone every year;
- Break up with cigarettes, e-cigarettes, vaping. Don't drink to excess, and don't do drugs;
- Break up with soft drinks and energy drinks;
- Break up with junk food, fast food, and highly processed food that makes you sick, contributes to obesity, and wastes your money;
- Break up with social media, *please*;
- Break up with television and avoid advertising that encourages you to purchase things you don't need;
- Break up with habitual shopping. Look at your calendar and select four days a year to shop online, and four days a year to shop at brick and mortar stores to buy non-essential items like clothing, shoes, and accessories. Make a list of what you need and wait for your shopping dates to come up. Know the items you're going to buy and buy only those items. Buy only what you need, and set a spending limit of $100.00 for each of the 8 shopping days in the year. (Exception: back to school wardrobe. See 'The Short List'.)

More Challenging Break Ups often take more time to consider, implement, and honor over the long term. That's because they include beauty products and clothing. Ouch! I didn't say this break up would be pleasant. I didn't say it would be painless. I did say it would be beneficial to you in the long run. *Clutch the pearls, dahling.* This is going to be difficult for both of us…but mostly for you.

The Break Up with Make Up

Let's discuss breaking up with unnecessary beauty products and the companies that put their corporate profits before their customers' health. Women are the target market, the dominant demographic, and the driving force behind the 50 billion dollar a year beauty products industry. The products are marketed to them as 'personal care', implying that these products are a necessity. Most are not.

While we've touched on the health hazards of many beauty products, we should also address the financial impact. One of the biggest drains on a woman's budget is the constant purchase of beauty products. This expenditure makes money management difficult. Women have billions of advertising and marketing dollars directed at them persuading them to spend money on beauty products and services that *they do not need.*

Seeing certain products or services as 'not necessary' can be challenging. Women have been brainwashed to believe that they actually do 'need' these things and 'must' have them. (Women are not alone in being brainwashed by advertising: I see plenty of metropolitan men driving big, burly pick-up trucks they've seen advertised on television. The closest some of them get to going 'off road' is when they pull up to valet parking.)

It's not just advertising and marketing that reinforce this 'need' belief associated with beauty products. It's the formative experiences of childhood and adolescence: watching your mother, grandmother, sisters, aunts, and friends apply makeup and share advice about it. It's almost a 'rite of passage' which many women include in their memories of what they think of as 'growing up' and 'life'.

What you need to remember as well is that your mother and grandmother were probably very selective about purchasing makeup and parting with their hard-earned and well-managed money. Cosmetics for previous generations were a luxury. Women rarely owned more than two of any particular item: a compact, a tube of lipstick, hand or face cream, and some lotion. That was about it, and they used all of it before they purchased more.

Today, many women can't imagine living without an abundance of these products. They're just a part of daily existence—routine and essential.

I have some shocking news for you: food and shelter are essential. Everything else is optional. This seemingly hardcore concept is foreign to many people, but when you endure an extended period of limited resources, you will learn the truth in it. Your life can go on just fine without television, designer labels, 'accessories', four-dollar coffees, overpriced manicures, and many beauty products. Again, you're going to have to do your own personal calculations as to how overspending on beauty products impacts your personal bottom line and your progress toward financial independence.

You also must weigh its health impact, as we've discussed. Foundations and powders applied all over your face just clog your pores and set you up to purchase even more products to get your skin clean and healthy again. Be aware that your skin is your body's largest organ. It absorbs up to 60% of whatever you put on it. When chemicals are absorbed through the pores of your face, those chemicals enter your bloodstream. Think about that.

Note: if you need some color in your cheeks, skip the rouge and exercise on a regular basis. Get the blood flowing. If you want to avoid wrinkles, avoid cigarettes, excessive alcohol consumption, and overexposure to the sun.

Anti-aging creams, face powders and foundations, eye-shadow, lipstick, blushes, mascara, nail polish, nail polish remover, face primer, hair, hair, and more hair products—the list is long and the costs add up, especially for women trying to get ahead. Trim your shopping list.

I support you doing things that make you feel beautiful, that make you feel more confident, that make you feel more empowered. However, I would encourage you to seek those positive feelings through education, exercise, and effort first. Then turn to cosmetics to only enhance the inner beauty and wisdom that are yours. Know your value, then spend your hard-earned money wisely. Remember the words of Bob Marley, who said, 'A smile is the most beautiful curve on a woman's body.' I'd add that it's also the most beautiful thing she can put on her face.

The good news about this break up is that there really are 'a lot of other fish in the sea', i.e., other companies that you can look at and perhaps start a relationship with. These are cosmetics companies often owned and operated by women (a total of 43 as of this writing). They are also companies that have done serious work to offer their customers products at a greater value with higher health and safety standards. Some of these companies include:

Deborah Lippman—Founded by celebrity manicurist Deborah Lippman, the beauty company that bears her name is one of the most renowned in the world.

Charlotte Tilbury—From age 13, Charlotte Tilbury knew she wanted to work in the beauty industry. After training at the Glauca Rossi School of Makeup in London, Tilbury jumped into the world of makeup. Now, her brand is a household name.

Honest Beauty—Actress Jessica Alba founded Honest Beauty when she saw a need for responsible, quality products with maximum ingredient transparency.

Edible Beauty—The naturopath and nutritionist Anna Mitsios launched Edible Beauty with the sole intention of creating a luxury botanic brand that is equally safe and effective. Anna's strong belief in the natural power of herbs is evident in her formulas.

It's A 10 Haircare—Founder Carolyn Aronson made history as the CEO of the first indie hair care brand to land a national Super Bowl ad. She also founded Kyana's Dream Foundation (in her daughter's honor) which focuses on providing emergency response for children in schools.

AveSeena—After spending 20 years researching the effects of estrogenic and endocrine disrupting chemicals on the immune system, Dr. Ebru Karpuzoglu decided to pour her scientific discoveries into a 100% nature-derived skin care brand.

MaBrook & Co—In 2014, Aliya Dhalla launched her brand of 100% natural and aluminum-free deodorant. The Clean Deodorant fully harnesses the benefits of activated charcoal, baking soda, and sweet floral scents.

Fact—Founder Cassy Burnside has launched her brand of Paleo-friendly and cruelty-free skin care products that are packaged and formulated for women on the go.

Aphorism Skincare—After battling a rare but curable cancer, Urvashi Singh set out on a journey to research the links between the toxic chemicals in cosmetics and disease triggers. This led her to launch a luxurious line of non-toxic skin care products.

Also consider Joshua Onysko's Pangea Organics, Dr. David Bronner's Magic Soaps, Greg Starkman's Innersense, and Olown N'djotehala's Alaffie. These are just a few companies to consider. Do your own research and find those that are best for you.

It's important to look at the beauty industry in political terms as well. While women purchase the vast majority of beauty products sold around the world and are often featured in the advertising and promotional campaigns for these products, they are vastly underrepresented in the executive ranks of these companies. As of this writing, women comprise less than 25% of the Boards of Directors of major beauty companies, and only 24% of their executive teams. Only 23 of the 500 largest cosmetics companies in the world have a woman as their CEO. The 6 most dominant corporations in the beauty industry all have men as CEO. These include L'Oreal, Estee Lauder, MAC, and Revlon.

A question you might ask yourself is this: with so many qualified female executives out there, why wouldn't the Board of Directors and the shareholders put a woman in charge of a company that sells most of its products to women?

It's important to remember that with beauty products—and all your purchasing choices—your dollars are your vote. Your dollars are your voice. In order to make informed choices, it's important to know which corporation owns your favorite brand or brands of makeup. There are reasons for this: one is to determine if a company is prioritizing the health of its customers. Another is to determine if a particular company is being a good corporate citizen.

Are they building strong communities by paying their employees fairly? Is their philosophy inclusive and their workforce diverse, both on the assembly line and in the executive ranks? Do they invest in a sustainable future? Are they attentive to their environmental footprint with regards to manufacturing, packaging, and distribution? Do they have 'green' goals? Do they participate consistently in charitable giving? (Not just feel-good publicity campaigns around charity events.)

It's also important to know if a company is selling two almost identical products, but marketing and pricing one 'brand' differently—and pricing it more expensively—than the other (the 'drugstore brand' and the 'luxury store' brand.) Some large corporations do this—produce essentially the same product and market it as two different products—to reach more customers in different demographics, saving the company money on production costs. Many times, only scents, textures, or packaging differentiate the products. This is the reason, for example, that *Lancome Eau Micellaire Douceur* and *L'Oréal Paris Skin Perfection 3 in 1 Purifying Micellar Solution* are almost identical products. The same corporate owner manufactures them with the same active ingredients. Only different 'brand names' and packaging separate the two in the eyes of the consumer.

It is true that some high-end products are made using more expensive ingredients and innovative technologies. However, the truth is they usually cost more because people expect expensive products to work much better than inexpensive ones and are, therefore, willing to pay more for them.

So, before you spend lots of money on a luxury product, do a little research on the company and its line. Compare the luxury product line's ingredients to those of their less expensive sister brands. Make an objective, informed determination if the difference in the ingredients is really worth the difference in price. To make your initial research easier, we've provided a starter list of 'who owns what' in the cosmetics industry in an appendix in the back of this book. It is not comprehensive, and the information may change as companies buy and sell brands, but it will give you a bird's eye view of the landscape.

Having this information will preserve your health, encourage good corporate governance, and save you money. Hopefully, this will also help you see beauty products for what they are: a big, profitable industry.

THE 'RAGS TO RICHES' BREAK UP

Another huge Break Up that women may face on the road to better money management is ending the unnecessary purchase of clothes and shoes. Women who buy the latest fashions, this season's 'must-haves', may sacrifice potential savings and future financial independence for cheap garments that are made overseas in near slave-like conditions...many times by women who have even fewer options in life.

To further damage their financial prospects, they may buy these items using credit cards. These credit card balances are rarely paid off at the end of the month. Double-digit interest is paid by the women who made the purchases, further adding to the 'real cost' of the item they purchased...even if it was 'on sale'.

Other women may do this, but you don't have to do this. An Old Money Gal never does this. Love and value yourself enough to be disciplined with regards to shopping for clothes. Purchase classic pieces—blouses, skirts, pants, jackets—that mix and match well. When you have the money, create variety with purchases of quality shoes, colorful scarves, and well-made purses that will last you a lifetime. Purchase quality. Keep it simple. Keep it classic. Keep it traditional. I have said much of this before. I'm saying it again. That should tell you something.

THE BIG 'C' BREAK UP

The biggest Break Up decision you may face is the decision to not own a car. The feasibility of this choice will vary greatly, depending on where you live, the access you have to public transportation, the climate, your profession, and your physical ability to get from one place to another on foot.

However, if you want to fast-track your program to financial independence, it might be something to think about. In addition to the purchase price of a new car (and in *The Old Money Book* I recommend considering a used car first) there are the issues of gasoline, maintenance, insurance, and parking. All of these eat into your ability to set aside money at the end of the month.

Options are to use public transportation, walk, bicycle, or scooter to where you need to go, or make use of companies like Uber and Lyft to get a ride only when you really need it. Yes, not having a car can be inconvenient. Not having financial independence can be inconvenient, too.

Less Than The Best

There are plenty of other temptations on the consumer landscape attempting to persuade a woman to part with her hard-earned dollars. These choices can be categorized as 'less than the best' decisions that a woman can make. If they become habits, they can drain a woman of her discretionary income, subsequently reduce her savings rate and investment opportunities, and, again, directly impact her chances of financial independence. Be aware of some of these choices so they don't hold you back:

- Overpaying for personal care expenditures such as manicures and pedicures at salons. The alternative? Do it yourself.
- Mobile phones and electronic devices. The alternative? Keep the old phone. Maintain and protect your laptop. Avoid big screen televisions. Actually, avoid televisions. Watch TV series and movies online and avoid the commercials that try to persuade you to buy things you don't need. Keep a book handy. Read, read, read.
- Too many dinners out, too many 'happy hours', too many 'girls nights out', i.e., paying retail prices for food and liquor at restaurants and bars. This behavior is a time-tested and sure-fire way to burn through a lot of money and have nothing to show for it, except maybe a headache the morning after. The alternative? Invite the girls—and maybe some guys—to your apartment for a wine or single malt whiskey tasting event. Be creative. Make it fun. Use your imagination.

You may not even realize you're making these unnecessary expenditures, and how it adds up, or how they're limiting your choices and your future. Now you know. Get a handle on them and tweak your monthly spending. Be disciplined in your pursuit of financial freedom.

'If you can't do a thing then you must do that thing. Conquer.'

—Anonymous

The Absolute Worst

We just covered 'less than the best' choices you could make regarding expenditures, and you can easily see how these bad habits can impede your ability to manage your money wisely. There is also the category of 'absolutely the worst' decisions you can make that will really destroy your financial future. I'll list some very quickly:

- Substance abuse: nothing can wipe out a healthy balance sheet like a few months of drug or alcohol abuse, either by you or a member of your family. Look for and be willing to accept help if you need it.
- Legal trouble: which may be brought on by the substance abuse, or simply stupid criminal activity, divorce (see *The Old Money Guide To Marriage*), choosing the wrong person to go into business with, or anything else that puts you in the crosshairs of the law and in need of lawyers. Civil lawsuits often fall in this category as well. Even if you 'win', the entire endeavor might be a losing proposition in terms of time lost, versus time spent doing something more worthwhile, as well as peace of mind.
- Unplanned pregnancy: getting pregnant before you've established a committed relationship with another person and before you've 'got your ducks in a row' is a reliable way to throw your finances—and future—into a tailspin. Remember: egg plus sperm equals baby. It's not an accident. I've said this before.
- Greed: nothing will ruin a profitable business or a solid investment strategy like greed. Being content with doing well and knowing when to sell are key to a high quality of life. As the old Wall Street proverb goes: Bears make money and bulls make money, but pigs get slaughtered.

In closing, know that the origins of waste—poor money management—are often confusion, apathy, and low self-esteem. You can remedy any and all of these conditions and walk yourself down a path of prudent financial choices, day in and day out. Regardless of your income, solid money management is key. Once you've mastered that, it's time to look at preserving what you've acquired and making it grow.

"There are two types of pain you will go through.
The pain of discipline and the pain of regret.
Discipline weighs ounces. Regret weighs tons."

–Jim Rohn

Exemplar – Barbara Jordan

Born and raised in a poor black neighborhood in Houston, Texas, Barbara Jordan was the daughter of a Baptist minister.

Encouraged by her parents to strive for academic excellence, she graduated with honors from her high school in Houston. Prohibited from attending the University of Texas at Austin due to segregation policies then in place, in 1956 Ms. Jordan graduated from Texas Southern University. She then continued her studies at Boston University School of Law.

After earning her degree, she returned to Texas and set up her law practice. Soon thereafter, Ms. Jordan became active in politics, campaigning for the 1960 Democratic presidential ticket of John F. Kennedy and fellow Texan Lyndon B. Johnson.

In 1962, Ms. Jordan launched her first bid for public office, campaigning for a seat in the Texas legislature. In 1966, after two unsuccessful bids, Ms. Jordan became the first African American woman in the Texas legislature. She was then elected to the Texas Senate in 1968.

In 1972, she ran for national office, becoming the first black woman elected to Congress from the South. While in Congress, Ms. Jordan gained national prominence, her powerful, measured, and compelling voice echoing through the chambers as she called for the impeachment of President Nixon during the Watergate hearings.

A strong supporter of the Equal Rights Amendment, she worked tirelessly for legislation against racial discrimination, and helped establish voting rights for non-English-speaking citizens.

After a storied career in politics in Washington, DC, she returned to the University of Texas, 30 years after she was denied admission as a student. This time, she walked onto campus as an adjunct professor, thank you very much, and taught ethics.

Look to Barbara Jordan as a life well-lived in her public service.

"You have got to be able to love yourself – love yourself strongly, and not let anybody disabuse you of your self-respect."

—Barbara Jordan

"The will to succeed is important.
The will to prepare is key."

—Joe Paterno

May 16, 2017—Larrasoana, Spain

CHAPTER 17

To Have and To Hold

So far, we've addressed the acquisition of material wealth and the management of money once you've received it. Now let's address preservation and growth as the final aspect of financial independence. This is done through saving money, which you should always do, and investing money, which you may choose to do.

'Investing' is the acquisition of income-producing assets that—you hope—increase in value over time. Some women choose investments that increase in value over time, but do not pay regular cash dividends. This means a woman would only profit if she sold her investment (shares of stock or land, for example) at a higher price than her purchase price sometime in the future.

If you have an ample source of income from your job or profession, you may be content to invest in an asset that is only expected to increase in value over time and does not pay dividends, interest, or put money in your pocket every month in some way. You may be comfortable with assets that you cannot liquidate quickly. You may also be comfortable with 'profits' that appear only on paper, like stocks, but which might have less value tomorrow based on circumstances you do not control. (Recent examples include stock prices fluctuating wildly based on the erratic behavior of a company's CEO and a company's involvement in a political scandal.)

Many women invest this way. Other women like assets that put money in their pockets every month and that they can liquidate quickly if necessary. At the very least, they like assets that they can borrow against or use as collateral to acquire other assets. This allows them to preserve their cash and stack their investments.

It is your mission to spend the time, do the research, ask the hard questions, and decide upon the investment strategy, philosophy, asset, or advisor that works for you. Do this only after long hours educating yourself and thinking about it. Remember that it is passive income from investments that enables a woman to be independent, to have options, and to do what she wants to do with her time as her financial needs are consistently met.

Know this also: you will face an inevitable risk/reward ratio for any investment you consider. The potential risk and the potential reward will be equal in all instances. Risk is part of even the most conservative investments. However, investing in income-producing assets can provide a second source of income. By choosing to invest and invest wisely, women can reduce one of the biggest risks they face today—having only one source of income, namely, a job. A second source of income from an asset could be a lifesaver if a woman loses her job or is otherwise unable to work.

I want to state again clearly that I don't give investment advice about stocks or bonds in general or in particular, real estate, or any other asset class. There are qualified professionals who commit their lives to devising investment strategies and locating investment opportunities that will pay dividends consistently and increase in value over time. Seek them out if you wish. Here are some general, overall thoughts I'll offer, at the risk of repeating myself, not because I don't remember what I wrote, but because I want you to remember what you've read:

First, your work will be to adopt a *philosophy of investing* that suits your personality and your goals. This means, simply, how much risk can you tolerate and how much liquidity do you need? The risk/reward ratio is like gravity: you just can't get away from it, and God help you if you try to defy it. Sooner or later, it will take hold and show you the nature of the law. The law is: the potential reward is equal to the potential risk. Accept this.

Second, you're going to have to do *research* about investment opportunities yourself. The quality of your information will be the quality of your knowledge, which will in turn affect the quality of your decisions and the quality of your return on investment. If you read glossy, mass-marketed magazines or blogs by who-knows-who to get investment advice, be prepared for lackluster returns or gasp-inducing losses.

Third, you will probably, at some point, be well-served to enlist the help of a professional investment advisor. Referrals from an OMG (Old Money Gal or Old Money Guy) are best in this regard. Look for someone with a track record of results, not a briefcase full of promises and a good haircut. Look for someone who doesn't get a commission on every trade. You want to make sure your investment advisor and certified pubic accountant are focused on *increasing your net worth and limiting your tax liability* over the long term. Be willing to pay a premium for expert advice regarding these issues.

Fourth, you'll want to make sure that you have a *diversified portfolio* so that if things go badly in one investment class, you have another asset (or three) that will increase in value, or at least hold its own.

Again, know that passive income from investments enables a woman to be independent, to have options, and to do what she wants to do with her time as her financial needs are consistently met. The decision of what to invest in, how much to invest, and when to liquidate investments is completely your own.

The more you earn, the greater your percentage of savings-to-income should be. If you're saving 10% of your income as an assistant, when you get promoted to manager, you should consider saving 20%. As you acquire assets, it is wise to take the income from those assets (or profit from their sale) and reinvest it in acquiring more assets. Stack your assets. Again, consider diversifying your assets at some point. Do the research. Learn what works for you. Be deliberate. Be determined. Failure to prepare, Benjamin Franklin said, is preparing for failure.

Have your job and your assets generating income for you. Have your 'emergency fund' of 6 months to a year of living expenses in the bank. Then, consider starting a business on the side to bring in more income. Remember: money is power, especially for women.

Old Money Investing

We've discussed the Old Money Gal who lives quite comfortably from the interest, rental, royalty, or dividend income from her investments. She lives below her means and does not touch the 'principal' amount of capital that is invested. This is the 'goose that lays the golden eggs'. When an Old Money Gal is 'financially independent', she can do what she wants with her time and have her financial needs met by the cash she has on hand and by investments that provide what is called 'passive income'.

This 'passive income' is called that because it is not dependent upon 'active' involvement, such as work or performance by her, in order for her to receive the income. The only requirement of a woman with passive income is to wake up in the morning. The passive income arrives regardless of whether or not she makes any effort that day, that week, that month, or that year. Investments that provide passive income to their Optimum Independence owners include:

- dividends from stocks, bonds, and annuities;
- rental income from residential properties such as apartment buildings; commercial properties such as office buildings or parking lots; or agricultural properties, such as farmland or grazing land;
- royalties from intellectual properties such as books, photographs, songwriter and/or music publishing rights, films, patents, trademarks, and technological innovations;
- investment in an existing, profitable business as a 'silent partner', i.e., a partner who has only a financial investment, not day-to-day work responsibilities.

If a financially independent woman's assets far exceed her needs (and even her wants) she is considered 'wealthy'. Luxuries can be acquired and enjoyed without concern for future financial well-being. Generosity is second nature. A world of possibilities to do well—and do good—are open to her.

The Old Money Gal recognizes the true value of money, its power, and the freedom it brings. Therefore, she prioritizes earning and spending differently than most of the population. She recognizes the true value of health and education and prioritizes them as a means to maximize her quality of life and earning potential. She spends less on 'goods and services' (material things) and prioritizes acquiring 'assets' (investments) and enjoying experiences.

When goods and services are purchased, the Old Money Gal is in a position to acquire the best and pay cash for it. This is the only true way to 'save' money. Buying the best, of course, can have different meanings for different people, but for the Old Money Gal it means this: knowing the difference between what is affordable and what is cheap. Affordable is maintaining your standard within your budget. Cheap is 'buy one get one free', which means you're overpaying in the first place for something that probably is of poor quality.

Spending habits are prioritized with an eye on the future. For example, some women work each week and get paid. They take some of the money they make, go to a restaurant, and enjoy a meal out. The Old Money Gal takes that same amount of discretionary income and saves it. Over time, she acquires enough money to buy a restaurant, creates an asset that brings her money each month, and has the option to let someone else do the cooking for once.

Very often, what people spend their money on each month over time determines in the end whether they end up 'rich' or 'poor'. Consumer products...poor. Assets... rich.

The Old Money Gal lives below her means, limits consumer spending, and uses the often hefty balance of her funds to acquire assets that generate the income she lives on.

To be clear, the days of an Old Money Gal—or any woman—remaining blissfully ignorant about her or her family's finances are long gone. There's no, 'Oh, my husband looks after all that,' anymore. The Ladies Who Lunch are now the Ladies Who Know Where Every Dime Is. As a woman on the road to financial independence, emulate the behavior of those who are where you want to be.

Things To Remember

Buy the best. You'll only cry once.

When you're old enough to vote and drive, you're old enough to stop blaming your parents for bad guidance, holding you back, or generally messing up your life.

Your parents' money, position, or accomplishments are not yours to spend or leverage. Be your own person. Blaze your own trail.

Compromises generally satisfy no one.

Be a guardian of the progress other women have made before you. Be a guide to other women who come after you.

Moving beyond small dreams will take you beyond small problems.

Treat yourself like a corporation—one that should make a profit each month. Plan performance bonuses for yourself, as the CEO, to mark the achievement of certain savings and investment goals. Take a trip. Enjoy a night out at an expensive restaurant with someone special. Invest in luxurious bed linens. Be creative. It's fine to increase the celebration as the accomplishment increases. Again: *Plan. Work. Earn. Save. Invest. Spend.* Keep these things in this order.

In addition to money management questions, ask yourself time management questions like: how much time are you spending commuting to and from work every day? If it's more than an hour each way, consider moving closer to your job. That's hours of your life sitting in traffic or on the train.

In the words of Benjamin Franklin, 'Lost time is never found again.' Embrace that concept. Old Money Gals do.

Exemplar – Mae Jemison

Born in 1956, in Decatur, Alabama, the young Mae Jemison wanted to be a scientist, and she worked hard to achieve her goals. A brilliant student, she entered Stanford University on a National Achievement Scholarship at the age of 16. Dr. Jemison received a Bachelor of Science degree in chemical engineering in 1977 and then attended Cornell University Medical College. While there, she studied in Cuba and Kenya and worked at a Cambodian refugee camp in Thailand.

She did her internship at Los Angeles County/USC Medical Center and worked as a general practitioner, then did research as the Peace Corps medical officer for Sierra Leone and Liberia.

In 1985, she decided to follow her dream of going into space and applied for admission to NASA's astronaut training program. The Challenger disaster of 1986 stalled the selection process, but a year later she reapplied and was one of 15 candidates chosen.

On June 4, 1987, Dr. Jemison became the first African-American woman to be admitted into the NASA astronaut training program. After more than a year of intense training, she became the first African-American woman astronaut. Earning the title of science mission specialist, she would be responsible for conducting crew-related scientific experiments on the space shuttle.

When her spacecraft launched in 1992, with six other astronauts on board, she became the first African-American woman in space.

After leaving NASA in 1993, Dr. Jemison accepted a teaching fellowship at Dartmouth College, and founded the Jemison Group, an advanced technology company.

Space, the final frontier. Mae Jemison has boldly gone there. If you're interested in space exploration, learn more about her life.

"The best way to make a dream come true is to wake up."

—Mae Jemison

"Embrace discomfort for mastery."

—Anonymous

May 22, 2017—Navarrette, Spain

CHAPTER 18

'First' Ladies

This final chapter recognizes women who were 'firsts' in their fields of endeavor. They include politicians and business women, athletes and adventurers. These women shattered glass ceilings and broke down barriers. They may have been among the 'first' to do great things in our world, but they certainly won't be the last.

First Woman to make a billion dollars—Yoshiko Shinohara

Born in Japan during World War II, Ms. Shinohara had a difficult childhood. Still, she managed to graduate high school and get work as a secretary. Having witnessed her widowed mother struggle to make ends meet, she decided to help other women. Her temp agency, *Temp Holdings*, gave Japanese women employment opportunities. Started in her one-bedroom apartment, revenues this year will top $6.5 billion.

First Woman to travel into space—Valentina Tereshkova

At 26 years of age the former textile worker and amateur sky diver became the first woman to travel into space and was the fifth cosmonaut to go into the Earth's orbit. She was selected from over four hundred applicants to pilot Vostok 6. Although plans were in place for further woman-led flights into space, Valentina's female cosmonaut group was dissolved in 1969. It would be almost 20 years before the second woman, Svetlana Savitskaya, made the journey.

First Woman to run for President of the United States—Victoria Woodhull

Although little known today, American suffragist Victoria Woodhull was the first woman to ever run for President of the United States in 1872. She was also one of the first women to open a Wall Street brokerage firm and made a fortune with her sister on the New York Stock Exchange.

First Woman to win an Olympic Gold medal—Charlotte Cooper

Five times Wimbledon singles champion, Charlotte Cooper became the first female to win an Olympic Gold Medal (for tennis) in 1900.

First African American Woman to win a Grand Slam Title in tennis—Althea Gibson

Ms. Gibson not only won 11 Grand Slam tournaments in tennis during her career, she was the first black woman to play on the women's professional golf tour.

First Woman to lead a Muslim state—Benazir Bhutto

As the 11th prime minister of Pakistan, Benazir Bhutto became the first woman to head a Muslim state in 1988. She ended military dictatorship in the country and was noted for her battle for women's rights. She was assassinated in 2007.

First Woman elected to British Parliament—Countess Constance Markiewicz

Irish revolutionary Countess Constance Markiewicz was the first woman ever to be elected to England's House of Commons. She rejected the position in protest, but later became the first woman to serve in a cabinet position, as Minister of Labour, in 1919.

First Woman to hold national office in the US—Jeannette Rankin.

Elected to the U.S. Congress in 1916, she believed that the corruption and dysfunction of the US government was a result of the lack of participation by women. During a disarmament conference, she famously declared that 'the peace problem is a women's problem.' Working tirelessly for more than 60 years, she championed gender equality and was instrumental in initiating the legislation that became the 19th Constitutional Amendment, granting unrestricted voting rights to women.

First Woman to swim across the English Channel—Gertrude Ederle

In 1926, American Gertrude Ederle, dubbed "Queen of the Waves", became the first woman to swim across the English Channel.

First Woman to fly a helicopter, rocket plane, and a jet fighter—Hanna Reitsch

German aviator Hanna Reitsch set over forty aviation altitude and endurance records during her career in the 1930s and 40s—and was the first woman to fly a helicopter, a rocket plane, and a jet fighter.

First Woman to break the sound barrier—Jacqueline Cochran

Pioneer Jacqueline Cochran was the first woman to break the sound barrier in flight on May 18, 1953, in a Canadair Sabre jet.

First Woman to be head of a government—Sirimavo Bandaranaike

Sri Lankan politician Sirimavo Bandaranaike was the world's first female head of government, serving as Prime Minister of Ceylon and Sri Lanka three times, 1960–65, 1970–77 and 1994–2000, and a long-time leader of the Sri Lanka Freedom Party.

First Woman to climb Everest -Junko Tabei

On May 16,1975, Junko Tabei, a mountaineer from Japan, became the first woman to reach the summit of Mount Everest. She was also the first woman to ascend all Seven Summits by climbing the highest peak on every continent on earth.

First Woman to be Prime Minister of Britain—Margaret Thatcher

Whatever you might think of her politics, the "Iron Lady" Margaret Thatcher was revolutionary as Britain's first female Prime Minister, serving from 1979 to 1990.

First Woman to complete a quadrathlon—Brenda Yule

In 1983, Brenda Yule became the first woman to complete a gruelling quadrathlon—involving swimming, kayaking, cycling and running.

First Woman to be Justice on the Supreme Court—Sandra Day O'Connor

American jurist Sandra Day O'Connor was the first female member of the Supreme Court of the United States, appointed by President Reagan in 1981.

First Woman to win Academy Award for Best Director—Kathryn Bigelow

Kathryn Bigelow made history in 2009 when she became the first woman to receive the Academy Award for Best Director.

In 2018, women accomplished even more...

The First Native American Women elected to U.S. Congress—2018

Sharice Davids, a former White House Fellow from Kansas, is a member of the Ho-Chunk Nation. Ms. Davids will also be the first openly lesbian member of Congress. As a lawyer and a former mixed martial arts fighter, she should be ready for anything Washington DC throws at her.

Debra Haaland, a community activist, Ms. Haaland is a member of the Pueblo of Laguna Nation. She was elected to a two-year term as the Chair of the Democratic Party of New Mexico in April 2015. During her tenure, New Mexico Democrats regained control of the New Mexico House of Representatives.

The First Muslim American Women elected to U.S. Congress—2018

Ilhan Omar, a Democratic state legislator in Minnesota, will also be the first Somali-American to serve in Congress. She has called for gun control, single-payer health care and a pathway to citizenship for undocumented immigrants.

Rashida Tlaib, a Democratic former state legislator in Michigan, and a Palestinian-American attorney, has championed Medicare for All, a $15 minimum wage, and abolishing the federal agency Immigration and Customs Enforcement.

First Woman Of Color from Massachusetts elected to the U.S. Congress—2018

Ayanna Pressley will become the first African-American woman to represent citizens of Massachusetts in Congress. Her opponent was a 10-term incumbent. Ms. Pressley has vowed to pursue "activist leadership" to advance a progressive agenda.

First Woman of Color from Connecticut elected to the U.S. Congress—2018

Jahana Hayes, a school district administrator in Waterbury, Conn., will become the first African-American woman to represent citizens from Connecticut in

Congress. Ms. Hayes, a Democrat, was a celebrated former history teacher who was chosen as the National Teacher of the Year in 2016.

First Twenty-Something's elected to the U.S. Congress—2018

Alexandria Ocasio-Cortez, 29, will be the youngest woman to ever serve in Congress. Ms. Ocasio-Cortez became an overnight sensation in the summer of 2018 after her upset primary defeat of Rep. Joe Crowley, a 10-term incumbent who was also the No. 4 ranking Democrat in the House of Representatives. The November general election made her victory in New York's 14th Congressional District official.

Abby Finkenauer, Iowa's first congresswoman and one of the nation's youngest. The Hawkeye State has never sent a woman to the House—until now. Ms Finkenauer, a 29-year-old Democrat, served two terms as a state representative, defeated her Republican opponent. Although she is the same age as Ms. Ocasio-Cortez, Ms. Finkenaur will 30 in December of 2018, just weeks before her swearing in ceremony in January.

First Texas Latinas elected to U.S. Congress—2018

In the nearly 175 years since Texas joined the union, the state has sent more 300 representatives to Congress, but none have been Latina—until now. El Paso County Judge Veronica Escobar and Texas state Senator Sylvia Garcia of Houston won their congressional districts in the 2018 Mid-Term elections, and will represent those districts in 2019 when sworn into office .

First Woman elected to the U.S. Senate from Arizona—2018

Kyrsten Sinema will be Arizona's first female United States Senator when she's sworn in on January 3, 2019. She narrowly defeated her opponent, Martha McSally. Ms. McSally, notably, was the first woman pilot to fly combat missions for the United States Air Force and the first woman to lead a fighter squadron. So both are 'First' Ladies.

First Woman elected to the U.S. Senate From Tennessee—2018

Marsha Blackburn, a Republican, will be Tennessee's first female United States

Senator. She has the experience: she's an eight-term member of Congress representing Tennessee's Seventh Congressional District.

First Woman elected Governor of Maine—2018

Janet Mills was elected after nearly eight years of Maine being governed by Republican Gov. Paul LePage. The people of Maine replaced him, electing their first woman governor. Ms. Mills, a Democrat, previously served as Maine's attorney general.

Find your own inspiring 'First' Ladies, or become a 'First' Lady yourself.

"Truth is a bully we all pretend to like."

—David Roberts

May 21, 2017—Logrono, Spain

Conclusion

Mastering the fundamentals of a philosophy—Old Money or otherwise—is never easy. You are required to grasp the overall concepts and then apply them to the details of your daily life. It is often a hit-and-miss process, filled with instant epiphanies, exciting improvements, and enduring struggles.

The key to this mastering is to determine what motivates you. Is it a desire for success? A fear of failure? Whether it's either one—or both—make sure that you're operating from a definition of 'success' or 'failure' that is yours and yours alone. The world will happily and frequently attempt to dictate the terms and conditions of these two concepts to you, for you, if you don't establish your own.

Take it one step at a time, one issue at a time, one exercise at a time. The pleasant surprise for you is that you'll most likely see more than one benefit at a time: the progress you make in one area of your life always ripples with positive effect into another area.

Remember that the progress you make as a woman will, for the most part, reflect the goals you define, the strategies you conceive, and how effectively you implement them. Your progress will also be equal to your resolve, as a community and as an individual.

Remember that living the life of an Old Money Gal has less to do with money and everything to do with integrity and independence, consistency and consideration.

Remember, also, the tremendous power that lies in the word 'No.' I hope that you will use this word to reject obsolete beliefs, attitudes, customs, and laws that have held women back. In the sacred texts of India, time is referred to as 'all powerful' and 'world-destroying'. I hope you will think of the word 'No' as not being necessarily world-destroying, but 'world-changing'. 'No' is not only a complete sentence, it is a position. It is void of ambiguity and filled with substance. When you say 'No' and refuse to accept something that is unjust, and stand firm, the perpetrator of the injustice has no choice but to change their behavior toward you or risk losing their relationship with you.

Most of the time, men will change their behavior toward women rather than risk losing them. This applies in personal relationships with boyfriends and coworkers as well as in the public sector where the 'women's vote' is pivotal. It also applies in business, as women make all the purchasing decisions for themselves and most of the decisions for their families. You, as an individual and as a group, have tremendous power to change unacceptable behavior. All you have to do is say 'No.'

Conversely, it is my hope that you will also say 'Yes' and embrace every constructive possibility and partnership to advance, improve, and enrich your life…and our world. Women are often in a unique position to see things differently than men, more empathetically and more subtly.

We, as men, often seek women out in order to make our world a loving, civilized, and decent place. We, as a planet, now need women more than ever in leadership positions: our governments and corporations are in desperate need of a new vision, a nuanced perspective, and fresh intelligence.

More than a half century ago, a song by the legendary singer James Brown began, 'This is a man's world, but it would mean nothing, nothing without a woman or a girl...' While I'm not sure how much of the first part of that verse is still true today, I know in my heart that the second part will be true forever.

My last request is that you use the tools and Old Money philosophy presented in this book to lift yourself up, then to lift us up. Elevate your position in society, then elevate our discourse in politics. Give birth to a child if you wish, then give birth to a better world if you can.

In closing, I return to Goethe, who started with us on this journey, and let him have the final word:

"Dream no small dreams for they have no power to move the hearts of men."

I wish you all good things in abundance…

"I have decided to be happy because it is good for my health."

—VOLTAIRE

A Tibetan girl, deciding to be happy.
—Photographer unknown

Appendix of Cosmetics Companies: Who Owns What

Did you know who owns your favorite makeup? Here's a partial list, composed in 2018.

WALGREENS BOOTS ALLIANCE

- Boots
- Botanics
- Liz Earle
- No 7
- Soap & Glory
- Solution

AVON

- Avon Color
- Anew And Solutions
- Mark

BEIERSDORF

- Eucerin
- La Prairie
- Nivea

COTY

- Calvin Klein
- Davidoff
- Jill Sander
- Lancaster
- Opi
- Philosophy
- Rimmel London
- Sally Hansen
- Younique Cosmetics
- Wella

Also owns lots of brands of perfume including Sarah Jessica Parker, Jennifer Lopez, Kylie Minogue, David and Victoria Beckham, Marc Jacobs and Chloe

ESTEE-LAUDER

- Aerin
- Aramis
- Aveda
- Bobbi Brown
- Bumble and Bumble
- By Kilian
- Clinique
- Dauphin

- Donna Karan
- Estee Lauder
- Eyes by Design
- Flirt!
- Frederic Malle
- Glamglow
- Good Skin Labs
- Grassroots
- Jo Malone
- Kiton
- La Mer
- Lab Series
- Lab Series Skincare for men
- Le Labo
- MAC
- Michael Kors
- Missoni
- Mustang
- Ojon
- Origins
- Osier
- Prescriptive
- Rodin Olio Lusso
- Smashbox Cosmetics
- Tom Ford Beauty
- Tommy Hilfiger
- Too Faced
- Tory Burch

JOHNSON & JOHNSON

- Ambi skincare
- Aveeno
- Clean and Clear
- Johnsons
- Lubriderm
- Neutrogena
- Purpose
- Piz Buin
- RoC
- Rogaine
- Shower to shower
- Vendome

KAO

- Ban
- Bioré
- Curél
- Guhl
- Jergens
- John Frieda
- Kanebo
- Molton Brown

LOREAL

- Biotherm
- Cacharel
- Carol's Daughter
- Clarisonic
- Decleor
- Diesel
- EM Michelle Phan
- Essie
- Garnier
- Giorgio Armani
- Helena Rubinstein
- Innéov

- IT Cosmetics
- Kérastase
- Kiehl's
- L'Oréal Paris
- L'Oréal Professionnel
- La Roche-Posay
- Lancôme
- Matrix
- Maybelline New York
- Mizani
- NYX
- Pureology
- Ralph Lauren
- Redken
- Roger & Gallet
- Sanoflore
- Softsheen-Carson
- Shu Uemura
- SkinCeuticals
- Urban Decay
- Vichy Laboratoires
- Victor & Rolf
- Yves Saint Laurent Beaute

LVMH

- Moet Hennesy—Louis Vuitton
- Acqua di Parma
- Benefit
- Dior
- Fendi
- Fresh
- Givenchy
- Guerlain
- Kat Von D
- Kenzo
- La Brosse et Dupont
- Make up for ever
- Nude
- Ole Henriksen
- Perfumes Loewe
- Sephora

MANZANITO PARTNERS

- Byredo
- Diptyque
- Eve Lom
- Kevyn Aucoin
- Lipstick Queen
- Malin and Goetz
- SpaceNK

PROCTER AND GAMBLE

- Aussie
- Boss Black & Orange Fragrance + Skincare
- Braun
- Clairol
- Covergirl
- Gillette
- Gucci Fragrances
- Head and Shoulders
- Herbal Essences
- Infusium 23
- Lacoste Fragrances

- Max Factor
- Noxzema
- Olay
- Pantene
- Perfect 10
- SK-II
- Venus
- Also owns lots of fragrances including Boss, Hugo and Valentino

REVLON

- Almay
- CND
- Elizabeth Arden
- Revlon
- Sinful Colors
- Ultima 2

SHISIDO

- Bare Minerals
- Clé De Peau
- Dolce & Gabbana
- Elie Saab
- Issey Miyake
- JPG
- Laura Mercier
- Majolica Majorca
- Narciso Rodriguez
- Nars
- ReVive
- Serge Lutens
- Shiseido

UNILEVER

- Axe
- Clear
- Dermalogica
- Dove
- Kate Somerville
- Lux
- Murad
- Pears
- Ponds
- Rexona
- St Ives
- Sunsilk
- Tony & Guy
- TRESemmé
- Vaseline

About the Author

After turning down a full scholarship to Brown University following high school graduation, Byron Tully left his family home in Houston, Texas, and moved to Los Angeles.

He took a job cleaning toilets at the Hard Rock Cafe. Six months later, he was promoted to Assistant Art Director, responsible for collecting and cataloguing the largest collection of rock and roll memorabilia in the world. Shortly thereafter, he penned a screenplay. The script landed him a literary agent and was quickly optioned by a Hollywood producer.

Byron continued to write for the industry throughout the Financial Crisis of 2007, when he watched many seemingly affluent friends and colleagues in Los Angeles struggle to pay their bills and keep their homes. In an effort to uncover why modest, discreet Old Money families (i.e., families who've enjoyed three generations of wealth or more) remained relatively unscathed by the Recession, he travelled to Boston, London, Paris, and Geneva. There, he researched and interviewed the 'quiet upper class' and learned in detail about their way of life.

As a result of this 'armchair anthropology', as he calls it, Byron wrote *The Old Money Book* in 2013, to immediate popular success. The book details the Core Values that privileged individuals and families often adhere to and chronicles how they prioritize their spending. *The Old Money Guide To Marriage* quickly followed, articulating the philosophy and strategies used by the Upper Class as they date, get engaged, and marry.

Old Money, New Woman: How To Manage Your Money and Your Life, published in 2019, is Byron's latest nonfiction work. This timely and informative 'life manual' for women reveals the little-known traditions and practices of upper class ladies and how they can be used by any woman to achieve financial independence and personal fulfillment.

Today, Byron curates The Old Money Book blog (theoldmoneybook.com) which has been visited by over 1 million readers since 2014. His media appearances include WABC's Financial Quarterback radio show in New York City, as well as the Tea With Lily podcast with host Lily Mensah Yeboah in London.

As the grandson of a newspaper publisher and son of an oil industry executive, Byron constantly articulates and promotes Old Money Values to this generation and the next, hoping to bring ethical, enlightened thought and behavior to the modern world.

With his first novel due to be published in 2019, Byron continues to write for the entertainment industry. He lives in Europe with his wife, an Old Money Gal from Boston.

Additional Works by Byron Tully

The Old Money Book:
Secrets of America's Upper Class -
How To Live Better While Spending Less

The Old Money Guide To Marriage:
Getting It Right, Making It Last

The Hindu Way To Wealth:
My Private Conversations with One of India's Richest Men

How To Be Happy:
The Practical Guide to the Most Essential
and Overrated Pursuit of Your Life

Printed in Great Britain
by Amazon